HOW TO TEACH
MUSIC
TO CHILDREN

By

CLELLA LESTER PERKINS

**FORMERLY HEAD OF DEPARTMENT OF PUBLIC SCHOOL MUSIC
STATE NORMAL SCHOOL, LEWISTON, IDAHO
AND TEACHER OF MUSIC, CHICAGO HIGH SCHOOLS**

HALL & McCREARY COMPANY
CHICAGO

ACKNOWLEDGMENTS

The author acknowledges her indebtedness and expresses her appreciation to each and all of those who have so generously given time, constructive criticisms, suggestions, and other assistance in the preparation of this work. Appreciation is also expressed to many teachers in various schools who gave valuable assistance in trying out the methods and materials which have been used.

Among the many who have contributed to the book it is felt that special mention is due the following: to Mr. Delmar R. Dewey, Director of Training School of Oregon Normal School, Monmouth, Oregon, who first suggested the preparation of this book; to Dr. Preston Ware Orem who read the original manuscript and gave many valuable suggestions; to Mr. Frank Ames Power, formerly Director of Music Department of Fairmount College, Wichita, Kansas, for his inspirational teaching and permission to use the following songs which appear in the song section: *Marching, I Hear a Little Tapping, The Big Bad Mouse,* and *Lullaby;* to Miss Hazel Louise Brown, Harrison High School, Chicago, for helpful suggestions and the use of the words of the song entitled *A Sailor Dear;* and to Betty Brown Lamis, Librarian of Educational Music Bureau, Chicago, for special help in research work.

Grateful acknowledgment is also made to the following authors and publishers who have so kindly granted permission for the use of their copyrighted material: to Rand, McNally & Company for *A Thankful Song* by the author; to F. A. Owen Publishing Company of Dansville, New York, for *The Goblin Man* by Sallie G. Fitzgerald, *Old March Wind* by the author, and a special arrangement of *Rainbow Song* by Offenbach; to M. Hohner, Inc., for permission to quote freely from their book entitled "The Art of Playing the Harmonica"; to The Cable Company for *Boy Scout March;* to Eleanor Jewett and The Chicago Tribune for the poems *On Easter Eve* and *First Snow;* and to Clayton F. Summy Company for permission to make and use a simplified form of the part-song, *A Sailor Dear,* by the author.

CONTENTS

CONTENTS

Preface

This book is designed to aid all who teach music to children, especially the classroom teacher who has had little or no musical training and experience. While the impossibility of touching upon more than a few of the countless phases of music in such a book as this is recognized, it is believed that all the essentials necessary to equip the untrained teacher in music are provided and in addition much that the trained music supervisor will find valuable. Wherever it has been deemed advisable, illustrations are provided to simplify and clarify the text.

Certain matters that may seem obvious to the trained musician will be found to have been treated in considerable detail. This has been done because it has seemed best not to assume any knowledge of the rudiments of music or of the basic facts pertaining to appreciation lest the book fail of its primary purpose. The chapter on the fundamentals of music will be useful as a source of information by the teacher untrained in music and for review or reference by those who have had training.

The teaching procedures are not put forward as precise methods to be followed without deviation. Rather they are to be looked upon as suggestive. With the assistance they offer, the teacher will find it easy to devise procedures that will meet the special needs of her class. The Daily Lesson Plans in Chapter XIII will also prove a valuable aid in formulating a consistent program which will assure the most effective use of the time given to music.

The Value of Music

"The value of music is simply the value that is in all art—and it is a priceless value. It promises to bring to the world moods, broad states of feeling that are aspiring, lofty, pure, untroubled, unselfish. It promises to bring into education the neglected third dimension—height—in addition to the prevailing thickness and breadth;—to develop the powers of the individual so that he will react rightly to the call of far voices that are beyond and above the little world of man . . . . . . music holds more power than academic and vocational subjects for the enrichment, purification, and uplift of the spirit of man."

WILL EARHART

PART ONE

CHAPTER I

A Personal Word

◆————————————————————————————◆

IF YOU HAVE not been specially trained to teach music but are desirous of preparing yourself to teach it as a part of your regular school program, perhaps you feel a certain anxiety over the problems involved in presenting it adequately to your pupils. This new responsibility may seem especially difficult because of the intangible nature of music, the fact that it lies within the province of art, and perhaps most of all because of the prevailing opinion that a special and rather mysterious aptitude for it is a prime necessity. It cannot be doubted that an aptitude for a particular study or art is a great advantage and even essential if one is to become truly expert in a special field. On the other hand, the vast majority of successful teachers in elementary schools may have had little natural talent for history, mathematics, or grammar, but by means of a good working knowledge of these subjects and a grasp of pedagogical principles their presentation in an intelligent and efficient manner is made relatively easy. The same is true of music. You have only to give to music the same conscientious attention you give to other subjects.

Read this book as a whole. Unless you are familiar with the various aspects of music, it will be well for you to read this book as a whole before beginning a study of it section by section. While reading the several parts it should be kept in mind that there is a very close interrelationship between the various subjects treated and that no single one can be adequately understood and applied to teaching without a sense of this fundamental unity. Remember also that in teaching, many of the different phases of music, although dealt with separately herein, are taught concurrently. Most of the methods and procedures given will be quickly grasped because of your general knowledge of pedagogy and educational procedures in other lines.

Confidence is important in approaching this subject. A love or at least a liking for it will facilitate your progress immensely. Fortunately people who dislike music are rare. This is especially true of teachers and educators, because as a class they are keenly aware of the profound cultural, moral, and social benefits accruing to the individual and to society through the study of music. When one considers its extraordinary expressiveness, its universality, and the lofty nature of the feelings and sentiments aroused by it, its supremacy in the arts can scarcely be doubted. Music is really one of the most powerful forces in the unfoldment and development of personality, and this aspect of it makes it of particular value in the schools.

In recent years the advances made in psychology and physiology have made possible many wonderful revelations regarding the changes that take place in the individual on both the physical and spiritual planes under the influence of music. The inculcation of finer thought- and action-patterns is an outstanding effect of contact with the higher type of music. This is of course especially true of children whose natures are still sufficiently plastic to be more susceptible to such influences than adults. Therefore, you as a teacher of music may be assured that you are not engaged in teaching some quite worthless though pleasant diversion but a subject constructive in the highest degree which cultivates a concern with beauty not only in tonal relationships but in all phases of life.

Be a good listener. A most essential step in preparation for the successful teaching of music is to develop the ability to listen to music in an intelligent and discriminating manner. All that we can know or enjoy of the art must be apprehended aurally; therefore it is this faculty which should be the object of special concern. Be a good listener by taking advantage of every opportunity to hear good music. It makes little difference what the character of the music is, whether it be vocal or instrumental or whether you hear it by radio or in a concert hall. The important point is that it should involve all your powers of attention and receptivity. The most fruitful approach to any art is not through reading or hearing lectures about it but through direct experience. If you now enjoy poetry, drama, the dance, or beauty of line, form, and color, you already possess much of the esthetic feeling demanded for the appreciation of music and this feeling can be best cultivated by devoting at least as much time to the hearing of music of the better class as to the study of its theory and practice.

Establishing Cooperative Attitudes. The first step in the successful handling of a class is to secure the interest-attention of the children through a sympathetic enthusiastic attitude toward them and the subject you are teaching. The pupils should be made to feel that their school activities are essentially cooperative and that the teacher is only an adult member of the group and its appointed guide. The music period can do more to foster this intimate contact between pupils and teacher than any other single phase of school work. That such a feeling of mutual under-standing is extremely important in molding the child's attitude in all matters which pertain to his life both in school and out of it need not be argued.

It is natural for children to desire to sing and therefore the teacher will never lack a joyful alert response if the approach is made in the proper manner. This means that the spirit of the music period should be that of pleasure, inspiration, and recreation—never a dull monotonous routine.

All explanations and suggestions to the class should be made in the simplest manner possible and without the use of unnecessary words. The more concise the statement the better. Long phrases are apt to be too great a strain on the attention of children. Lead them as far as possible to discover facts and the meaning of symbols for themselves. The need for having names for certain kinds of notes for instance will not be felt by them until they have had considerable experience with music. In the same way if they have been taught to clap or march to the words "one, two, one, two," it will be easy for them much later to learn that one, two, one, two, represent two measures of two beats each. In short, the rule should always be "experience before knowledge."

The child should never be made to feel that he is learning or studying music but rather that he is *enjoying* music. This most desirable attitude will be a natural result of his acquaintance with music if the songs chosen for his use accord with child experiences and interests and are within his comprehension as regards words, rhythm, and design. The world of the child is full of wonder, beauty, and novelty with endless possibilities of delight and enchantment. Something of this must be felt by the teacher in her work if it is to become a genuine creative activity.

Class Discussion.   It should never be forgotten that the main objective of all educational effort is the *unfoldment* of the individual. The word unfoldment indicates a coming-out, drawing-out process rather than a put-ting-in process. In helping children to discover knowledge for themselves a reasonable amount of class discussion is desirable. The teacher should ask questions and encourage the pupils to question her. The questions of the teacher should be so framed that the pupils are led by an unconscious process of reasoning to find the proper answers. This method is capable of the greatest variety in approach and application and should be applied particularly to the cultivation of a fine sensitive response to the beauty of the songs sung. The teacher will need to help the children express many phases of their reactions and to make effective contrasts with other material used.

Public Performance.   It will be found useful in creating interest and enthusiasm among the children and their parents if occasional opportunities are provided for public performance. Group singing should be the out-standing feature of such events, but the teacher may allow the more talented of the children to sing or play solo numbers. The approval of teacher and parents is an important factor in securing desirable attitudes in children. They are inspired by expressions of confidence in their ability and by generous praise for work well done.

Equipment.   If you are fortunate enough to have a keyboard instrument in the classroom and are able to play it, you begin with a considerable advantage. Be sure that the instrument is kept in tune, and endeavor to inculcate in the children a desire to take care of it as community property and a source of pleasure for all. If there is no instrument and you are given the opportunity to select one, by all means get an instru-ment with which you can demonstrate best—a piano or organ, if you can play it—if not, select a phonograph and suitable records.

A pitch pipe and staff liner are indispensable.

The choice of a song book is of particular concern, because the appro-priateness and musical value of the songs are so important in determining the child's appreciation of music and the degree of his pleasure and stimu-lation. To be well suited for school use, a book should contain rote songs, observation songs, study songs, and songs for sight reading—some in unison and some in parts. It should also contain many songs for patriotic, sea-sonal, and devotional purposes.

Music Period.   The most rapid progress can be made only when the music period is a part of the regular daily routine of the school. If possible, the time allowed should be fifteen to twenty minutes. If a shorter period must be given, it is wiser to devote ten minutes each day than twenty minutes every other day. Music is an essential curricular activity, and irregularity in classes is apt to suggest unimportance.

A review of musical experiences and knowledge previously gained ought to be a part of each lesson. The rehearsal of these should be continued until they are felt and thoroughly understood.

The Lesson Plan. For the inexperienced teacher a suggested lesson plan is given here. Each class lesson should have as much variety as possible and great care should be taken to avoid tiring the children by drilling them too long on any one special phase. The teacher will not be able in many instances to present a perfectly balanced lesson every day, but if she will follow roughly the procedure outlined devoting not more than four or five minutes to each phase of the lesson she can secure excellent results.

1. Have the children sing a familiar song.
2. Begin the teaching of a new song.
3. Present some kind of rhythmic drill.
4. When the class has made sufficient progress, spend some time on the recognition of tone groups and give a short drill on note reading or pitch names. Vary this with dictation or ear-training.
5. Review songs learned in previous lessons.

Glee Club and Choir. As the children gain in ability, both interest and endeavor will be stimulated if a glee club or choir is organized. Only the best singers should be selected for these special groups with the understanding that others will be admitted as soon as they qualify for membership. There should be no "try-outs" that the pupils recognize as such. Four or five songs are selected from those which are sung best by the class as a whole and individual pupils are asked to sing them. In ungraded schools all the grades may sing together at first and for a time the teacher may humor the children's preference as to the songs they sing. The most talented are chosen to form the nucleus of the new group. The work of the choir or glee club should be an extension of the work done in the regular music period but with more attention given to matters of tone quality, nuance, articulation, and general expression than is possible with the larger group.

If the teacher finds it possible to do so, both glee club and choir may well be formed, the club smaller than the chorus as a whole, and the choir comprising only the best talent in the school. The value to the pupils and to the community of these musical activities cannot be over-estimated.

Objectives. The goals for which every teacher should strive are the following. These include all of the standard objectives for elementary grades adopted by the Music Educators' National Conference.

1. Every child shall have acquired the use of his singing voice and pleasure in song as a means of expression.
2. Every child shall have learned to enjoy music as something heard as well as something expressed.
3. Every child shall have awakened and vitalized within him a feeling of rhythm.
4. Every child shall have acquired a repertory of songs to be carried into the home and social life.
5. Every child shall have developed aural power to know by sound what he knows by sight, and vice versa, and therefore be able to sing at sight, using words, a unison song of hymn-tune grade; or using syllables, a two-part song of hymn-tune grade, and the easiest three-part songs; these to be in any key, to include any of the measures and rhythms in ordinary use, and any accidental signs and tones easily introduced. Also he shall have acquired a knowledge of the major and minor keys and their signatures.
6. Every child talented in musical performance shall have had an opportunity for its cultivation.
7. Every child shall have developed a love for the beautiful in music and acquired a taste in choosing the music to which he listens.
8. Every child shall have acquired an ability to appreciate the charm of design in music; to give an account of the salient features of construction in a standard composition after a few hearings of it; to identify at least the three-part song form from hearing it, and to recognize and give titles and composers of a reasonable number of standard vocal and instrumental compositions.

9. Above all, every child shall have arrived at a conception of music as one of the beautiful and fine things of his life.

The attainment of these objectives is possible in the average school having the necessary equipment if the skill and enthusiasm of the teacher are equal to the task and sufficient time is devoted to music each day.

CHAPTER II

The Singing Voice of the Child

THE MOST important instrument with which an instructor in school music deals is the singing voice of the child.

When the child first enters school he has had very little, if any, experience with his singing voice. At this initial and imitative period in the process of education the power to consciously produce tones and discriminate. between pitches is rudimentary. Children whose environment has been musical to any extent are usually more advanced in this respect than others. The average child must be patiently taught to sense pitch.

First of all, the greatest care should be taken to see that the tones are produced with the utmost freedom. There should be no conscious muscular control of the voice. All rigidity of muscles of the face, jaw, throat, or body must be avoided in order that the tones may be perfectly free and natural and the result of an unconscious adjustment of the vocal mechanism to the desired pitch. If these principles (which are the same for all grades) are followed, a perfectly loose throat, adequate breath support for sustained tones, and a natural control of the voice will be easily secured.

In the endeavor to avoid strain it is well with very young children to have them sing with only a medium degree of power—neither too loud nor too soft. All dynamics are of course relative. The range of tone power is naturally more restricted in very young children than in older children because of differences in physical development. Thus a dynamic range suitable for voices in the first three or four grades, of soft, medium loud, and loud, will correspond roughly to the very soft, soft, and medium loud of older children. In general it may be said that children should be taught to let their feeling about the expression of a song govern the quality of tone and range of dynamics employed. It is much better to secure a spontaneous reaction to the meaning of the words and music within the limits set by physique and good taste. Therefore allow the children reasonable freedom in the use of their voices.

An important consideration in promoting the production of good tones and an entire absence of physical strain is a clear enunciation of the words.

Range. The best results both in regard to musical effect and in preserving the natural freshness of quality in the voices of little children will be obtained if the songs in the early grades are kept within the limits of the treble staff.

Posture and Breathing. The physical and psychological benefits derived from the habit of maintaining correct posture is beyond question. Good singing and good posture are very intimately associated because the breath support necessary for singing purposes is difficult to secure unless the body is carried in the proper manner.

In order to breathe correctly the children should sit or stand in such a position that all muscular movement is free. Sitting or standing, the chest should be forward, the shoulders back, and the head up. When sitting, the feet should be flat on the floor, back erect but not leaning, and the body relaxed but not lounging or sprawling. If this posture is assumed, an easy buoyant attitude will result.

Do not make pupils "breath conscious" by too great emphasis upon this factor in singing, especially with the very young. With conceptions of beauty of tone and a buoyant posture free from constraint, good breathing will be more or less instinctive. Older students should be taught to sense and recognize the breathing points in a song. When the time for taking a breath at the end of the phrase is not provided for by means of a rest in the music, the last note should be given less than its normal value, so that the phrase following may begin exactly according to the beat.

The practice of singing will develop breath control better than any set exercise, the tone itself acting as a point of focus and control for the entire singing mechanism. If any exercise is needed, the following is one of the most effective: A slow easy intake of breath exhaled gently through pursed lips. This exercise may be made interesting to children by having them imitate the smelling of a flower and then gently blowing its petals away. In all singing care should be taken that there is no contraction of the mouth, throat, or body during the intake of breath.

Ability to Sing on Pitch. For the purpose of determining children's ability to sing on pitch have them imitate calls, using such simple intervals as the octave, fifth, fourth, and third. The use of these simple exercises will enable the teacher to determine which of the children need special attention. It is important that the model of tone which the teacher gives should always be one that is soft, round, and easily produced.

As the pupils become familiar with the pitches and intervals of the two-note calls, three- and four-word sentences in the form of a question and answer pattern may be used. The first of these exercises should be made up of tones of the tonic chord. Other tones may be added later. While the exact order of pitches sung by the teacher need not be followed by the children, the agreement in rhythm and tempo between question and answer should be reasonably accurate.

The following exercises are suggested:

1. The teacher calls the name of a pupil. He answers using the same tones. (See example below.) Other calls may be devised using the following tones: the teacher sings *do* (1)—*sol* (5), pupil sings the same; teacher *do* (8)—*sol* (5), child the same; teacher *sol* (5)—*do* (8), child the same; teacher *do* (1)—*mi* (3), child the same. Imitating the call of the cuckoo is also useful: the teacher sings *do* (8)—*la* (6), the child the same.

2. After a number of the children have been called and have answered, others may be tested by having them imitate the zoom of an airplane, the sound of wind, and the toot of a locomotive. These should be given on the same pitch given by the teacher.

3. The following are examples of suitable question and answer songs.

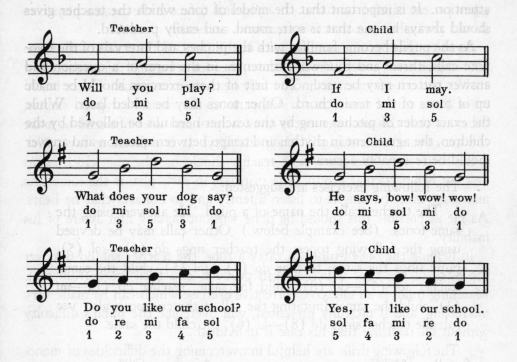

Teacher

Will you play?
do mi sol
1 3 5

Child

If I may.
do mi sol
1 3 5

Teacher

What does your dog say?
do mi sol mi do
1 3 5 3 1

Child

He says, bow! wow! wow!
do mi sol mi do
1 3 5 3 1

Teacher

Do you like our school?
do re mi fa sol
1 2 3 4 5

Child

Yes, I like our school.
sol fa mi re do
5 4 3 2 1

4. Another means of determining children's ability to recognize tone and sing on pitch is to have two children represent a bridge as in "London Bridge." The other children represent boats which want to pass under the bridge. The bridge is raised only when the correct signal whistle of the boat has been blown (sung). The teacher gives the tone of the whistle. When repeated correctly the bridge is raised and the boat is allowed to pass. This procedure is continued until each child has been tested on his ability to give the signal correctly.

Monotones. One of the first and most serious of the problems confronting the teacher is the training of monotones or "out-of-tuners" as they are called. They cannot sing a melody because they *seem* unable to vary the pitch. They differ in the pitches to which they cling, some being higher than others but all are alike in their inability to make appreciable variations. The difficulty is unusually due to a lack of coordination between the aural sense and the vocal mechanism. It can be remedied if given patient careful attention. If a physical defect is the cause a physician should prescribe the corrective treatment necessary.

Some teachers group out-of-tuners in the front of the room, with those who sing on pitch grouped back of them, the idea being that this arrangement enables the out-of-tuners to more easily hear the true pitch. Other teachers seat the out-of-tuners in various parts of the room near good singers, believing that this arrangement is more helpful and does not tend to make the out-of-tuners conscious of their inability. It is difficult to say which is the better way; therefore, each teacher should use the one which seems best for her particular group. The principle in each plan is the same; the monotone must be taught to listen intently and to imitate what he hears. As far as possible this should be done without making him aware of his inability.

In helping the out-of-tuner to carry a tune, the teacher should discover the pitch of the tone which he can produce, and then work from that. Matching tones is an effective corrective exercise which can be made very interesting, and if tactfully presented, will overcome the pupil's difficulty without his realizing that his case is individual.

The following drills are helpful in overcoming the difficulties of mono-tones:

1. Sing sustained tones rather slowly using the neutral syllable *loo*. Have the monotones hum or sing the pitches quite softly so that they may hear and follow the pitches and tones sung by the other children. This practice tends to develop the proper degree of concentration, the lack of which is often the cause of the monotones' difficulty.

2. The calls and other exercises on pages 10 and 11 will also be helpful in establishing ability to sing on pitch.

3. The following selections provide excellent song material for use in developing the pupil's pitch discrimination: *The Pumpkin and the Turkey*[1], *The Grocer and the Housewife*[2], *In September*[3], *Bobby Shafto*[4], and the chorus of *Lazy Robin*[5]. Use only the first phrase of each one and lead the children to *hear the tone*, then *think it*, and then *sing it*.

---

[1]p. 151, [2]p. 116, [3]p. 101, [4]p. 108, [5]p. 120.

The teacher indicates the direction of the tones of a melody by raising and lowering her hand with each change of pitch or draws lines on the blackboard at different elevations as the melody is sung.

Another effective device to establish the ability to vary the pitch of tone is to draw a ladder on the blackboard and have the children sing the ascending scale as the teacher points to the ascending steps of the ladder. Knowledge of the bodily movements required to ascend a ladder seems to form an association which gives the child the correct sense of the voice being lifted for each successive tone.

The Voices of Older Children. The singing voices of older children, those in the grades from four to eight, have the same general characteristics which the voices of younger children have and need to be treated in the same careful way. Some extension in the range of the songs used may be safely made by adding one or two notes below E and adding a note above the staff, thus extending the range from Middle C to G. Continue to keep the tones light in volume and quality. New phases of music are introduced and the material used is progressively more difficult.

The Changing Voice. During adolescence the voices of boys and girls mature rapidly. It is not as easy to sense the change taking place in the girl's voice as it is that taking place in the voice of the boy. The girl's voice becomes richer, but as a rule it does not change its register as from soprano to alto, or from alto to soprano. About the only problem with the voice of the girl is to keep it free from strain. Her tones should be produced with ease and should be of a light floating quality.

The voice of the boy during adolescence is a more difficult problem. Due to the rapid growth and development of the cartilages and the muscles of the larynx, he is not able to control the quality of his voice because of the deepening of the tones which is taking place. A wise and sympathetic teacher will explain to the adolescent boy that at his age certain changes are taking place in his vocal chords which will eventually lead to a change of voice. He should also be warned not to strain his voice in range or power during this period. Such an explanation will manifest a sympathetic understanding of the boy's difficulty and will result in keeping him inter-ested in his music during this period.

In some cases the boy loses his ability to sing during the period of change. Under such circumstances he should not be compelled to sing because it would be harmful for him to do so. However, this does not mean that he must not pay attention to such things as rhythm, note values, words, and similar phases of music which he can learn without participation in singing. As a matter of fact, there are but few boys who should be excused from singing, because one who cannot sing during this period is an exception rather than a rule. When the boy first senses a change he is startled and is likely to refrain from singing unless it is explained to him that the change is a natural one and that he is gradually acquiring a more mature voice. Quite often a boy's voice drops from a soprano to an alto, then down to a tenor. Later it may become a baritone or a bass. Usually the change takes place gradually. During the period of change it is often advisable to have the alto voice sing the tenor of a selection on the alto pitch. (See illustration below.) This will keep the voice within the limited range that is best suited for it. If boys' voices were treated more carefully at this important time, there would not be such a scarcity of good tenors. Through careless usage at this period many voices are forced permanently into too low a register.

Range of Young Voices

The "Break." Until overcome by training, the singing voice will often break, even when singing within its own range. This is particularly true of the changing voice. This break, however, should not be confused with the sudden change of tone that occurs in the voice of the adolescent who is unable to control it. The following exercises will be found useful in helping each voice to cover its range smoothly and without a noticeable break:

1. Have the boys sing the descending scale Bb (third line), A, Ab, and G. The girls should sing the descending scales E (fourth space), Eb, D, Db, and C.

2. Have the boy sopranos sing the alto part when the first huski-ness appears that usually marks the change.

3. At all times try to have both boys and girls sing with loose jaws and open mouths. A device to aid in this is to have the pupil place two of his fingers, one above the other, between his teeth, while singing *ah*. Such a procedure makes it physically impossible to tighten the throat muscles. The fuller and more pleasing tones that result usually surprise and delight the chil-dren.

CHAPTER III

Rote Singing

ROTE SINGING is singing by ear. Learning to sing by rote, therefore, is learning to sing by imitating what one hears and is the first important step in the musical development of the child. This method is a natural stepping stone to sight singing; and even in the upper grades where the students are able to read music, patriotic and national songs, pep songs, and other songs for special occasions are often taught by rote.

While rote singing is of great value and necessary in the beginning stages it is well to realize its limitations. The songs best adapted for this purpose are those in which the structure is comparatively simple with no intricate phrases or sequences which are not easily recognized by the ear. Songs which are more complicated in design require too much repetition to be suitable for rote teaching. In the field of school music the term "rote song" has come to mean a type of simple song adapted for use in the primary grades in which the word content is related directly to the child's experiences, impressions, and interests.

Preparation. In teaching a song by rote the teacher sings the selection in the correct tempo and with proper tone quality and interpretation. The children then sing the song repeating what they have heard. However, it will be found advantageous if the pupil's interest has first been awakened by a procedure of preparation somewhat as follows:

1. Sing, or play on the phonograph two or three songs the children have learned at home or in the kindergarten. The recollection of previous pleasant experiences with music helps to create a favorable attitude on the part of the pupils.

2. Bring out the story of the song so that the children will have a clear mental picture of the ideas it presents, and by appropriate questions, establish connections with their interests.

3. Teach the children to discover the meanings of any new or unfamiliar words or phrases found in the song.

4. If possible, correlate the song with some project or phase of school work in which the class has a part.

There are two methods of teaching rote songs in general use—the entire song method and the phrase method.* Both are successful. They are presented at this point.

The Entire Song Method. This method is considered the better for teaching short songs. The following simple procedure which may be varied to meet the needs of any particular group is quite generally followed:

1. The teacher sings the song. The children are then questioned regarding their understanding and enjoyment of it.
2. The teacher sings the song again while the children listen attentively. As imitation is the essential feature of rote singing, the teacher should be careful to sing the song each time with the best interpretation of which she is capable.
3. Gradually and naturally the children are led to join in the singing and little by little, as they learn it, the teacher withdraws her support and finally the children sing the song alone. How rapidly or how slowly the support is withdrawn depends upon the difficulty of the song and the alertness of the class.

Although the entire song method is generally accepted as best for teach- ing short songs, many use this method successfully for all songs taught by rote.

The Phrase Method. The phrase method of presenting rote songs is more suitable for longer songs. An effective procedure is the following:

1. The teacher sings the entire song while the class listens closely. She then gives her interpretation of it and makes sure that the song is understood by the class.
2. The teacher sings the first phrase; then the class repeats it.
3. The teacher sings the second and each succeeding phrase, one by one, and as each is finished it is repeated by the class until the entire song has been sung.
4. The teacher sings the entire song, and the class repeats it.

Extra drill should of course be given on the more difficult phrases or motives. At the discretion of the teacher two or more phrases which seem to form a unit may be presented together instead of but one phrase at a time.

*Teachers are urged to read *Educational Psychology* by E. H. Cameron, published by The Century Company, and give special attention to "Learning by Wholes and Parts," pages 257 and 258.

After the class has repeated the song the pupils may be called upon to express their reactions to it and their ideas as to how it might be interpreted differently. To these the teacher may add any comments and suggestions she deems advisable.

Teaching Rote Songs by Means of the Phonograph. For the teacher who feels that her voice is unsuited for singing, the phonograph is a valuable help. The use of this instrument with the following procedure will be found effective:

1. Tell the story of the song.
2. Play the song through while the children listen attentively.
3. Point out certain definite things for which the children should listen such as the melody, recurrences of phrases, rhythmic aspects, and general mood. Play the song once more and then question them to discover to what extent they have been able to concentrate upon the points mentioned.
4. Play the song and have the class hum the melody softly.
5. Read the words of the song and interpret any new words or unfamiliar word usage.
6. Have the children sing the words of the song softly with the phonograph.
7. Have them sing the song without the aid of the phonograph.

Selecting Rote Songs. In selecting rote songs the teacher should be guided by the following considerations:

1. That the song is of suitable length.
2. That it is of high quality both in text and music, and adapted to the ability and experiences of the children.
3. The possibilities of correlating the song with seasonal or project activities.

Rote songs for use in the lower grades should be short and easy. It is best to begin with songs built on the simple skips of the tonic chord. Later those containing diatonic (step-wise) progressions may be used. No song should be selected for class work unless it is within the proper range and contains elements of direct value in forwarding the musical and educational development of the child.

The children's enjoyment of simple folk songs and in particular traditional singing games, makes it advisable to include these types among the songs used in the early grades. However, the choice of such material ought by no means to be exclusive. The child's musical experience needs to be as broad as possible. In addition to songs especially appropriate to the grade, the teacher should select several that are suitable for carrying into upper grades, into the home, and into the community life.

Rote songs for the third, fourth, and fifth grades offer progressively finer material—songs that are lovely from the pupils' standpoint as well as from the musicians'. The child becomes more keenly aware of beauty in the design of the songs he sings and his emotional response is more varied.

Mention has already been made of the fact that in the upper grades many songs for special occasions as well as patriotic and national songs are often taught by rote. Songs that are true art songs and fairly complex in structure can also be taught in the intermediate grades by the same method. Many exquisite melodies are available from the song literature, operas, and oratorios of our greatest masters which are well adapted for use with upper class singers. Such selections are valuable in extending the range of knowledge and experience of the students and provide many avenues whereby a desire to enjoy more of the world's rich store of music is fostered.

Important Suggestions and Reminders. Consider the following carefully:

1. Know your song well before trying to teach it.
2. Do not guess at the pitch. Use your pitch pipe frequently as a means of testing the pitch.
3. Sing with the children only to illustrate, correct, or teach. After a song is learned do not sing with the children when leading, because singing with them tends to take away their independence.
4. For little children no instrumental accompaniment is needed. The unaccompanied song is especially appealing to children, and often the combined harmonies of an accompaniment are confusing to their inexperienced ears.
5. Every child should be given frequent opportunity to express himself individually by singing alone.

6. Do not teach songs that are musically too difficult and the texts of which are beyond the ready comprehension of the children. The songs, however, should always be sufficiently difficult to be interesting and to challenge the pupil's ability.

7. Do not busy yourself with other things while the class is singing. Keep your thought and interest with the class.

Teachers who cannot sing and yet are required to teach music often find it helpful to select a capable student as an assistant in teaching rote songs in the upper grades. The one chosen should possess a good general aptitude for music and a voice easily produced and true to pitch. By having the assistant observe the work of the music supervisor he or she will get a fairly clear understanding of the material to be presented and of the way it should be given to the class. If the teacher is in a non-supervised school the suggestions given in this book will enable her to carry on the music period successfully either with or without an assistant.

CHAPTER IV

Sight Singing

SIGHT SINGING is the vocal interpretation of musical notation at sight. This ability to identify the characters of written music and to interpret them by singing with the correct pitch and rhythm is the only adequate basis for an intelligent comprehension of the art. Learning to sing songs by rote only, cannot do much toward the cultivation of independence. Rote singers must constantly be led. Children should be taught to read and sing at sight just as soon as their progress indicates they are prepared for so doing. The first work in sight singing then goes hand in hand with rote singing. The teacher begins by placing upon a staff on the blackboard the notes of various songs the children have already learned by rote. Next, new songs used for sight singing purposes are introduced. They must of course be extremely simple. These are followed by selections of gradually increasing difficulty according to the progress and ability of the class.

The use of rote song material should, however, be continued long after note reading has been introduced, for it is very useful in learning new songs too difficult to be read easily. Once begun, sight singing should be stressed and diligently practiced in each lesson period.

The Sol-Fa Syllables. Despite many efforts made to secure a satisfactory substitute for the use of the sol-fa syllables in teaching sight singing, none has yet been found. The giving of definite names (do, re, me, fa, sol, la, ti, do) to the tones of a scale seems to aid children to establish a sense of the tonal relationships within a key more easily than any other method. Until some more practical and workable system is evolved these syllables will continue to be widely used. The study of solfeggio (sight singing by the sol-fa syllables) is still required in many higher institutions.

The most logical scale for beginning the use of the sol-fa syllables is the scale of C. Care should be taken that in singing the lowest tones the voices of the children are not strained.

After the syllables are introduced (usually early in the second grade) the work should be continued until the pupils have acquired a thorough understanding of them.

Singing by Position. The association of position on the staff with pitch is called *singing by position.* It is a "trial and error" method of learning and of itself can seldom lead to accurate sight reading.

Rote-to-Note Procedure. The expression "rote-to-note procedure" is used to designate ways and means of leading a child in his musical experience from rote singing to sight singing. This transition may be effected by either of two procedures which have been in general use for a number of years. One, known as the SCALE METHOD, is *inductive* (proceeding from the part to the whole) and consists largely of mechanical drill on the scale and exercises with the sol-fa syllables. Notes, rests, tone groups, sharps, and flats are carefully taught and gradually the students are led to apply this knowledge to song material. Such exercises carried on largely to the exclusion of song material become very dull and unpopular with both teachers and pupils. By judicious use this approach may be made interesting and profitable to the children, but the application of it should not be too intensive.

The other procedure, known as the SONG METHOD, is *deductive* (proceeding from the whole to the part). It is more modern and accords with present-day methods of teaching other subjects in the curriculum. The students, having learned a number of songs and acquired some feeling for rhythm, accent, and expression are led by means of a type of song, known as the Observation Song, into an analysis of songs as a whole. The song having been learned as a whole the pupils are led to discover the phrases, smaller groups, intervals, and the fundamental features of notation. Finally, by means of two other types, the Study Song and the Reading Song, the ability to read and sing at sight is developed.

The following gives the characteristics of the several types of songs mentioned in this procedure. Note that some songs may be classified under more than one heading, depending upon whether they have the required characteristics.

The **rote song** is one simple in structure, with a pleasing melody and a text which expresses ideas of interest to children. It is learned by ear and sung by imitation as outlined in Chapter III.

The **observation song**, or "pattern song" as it is sometimes called, like the rote song, is of simple structure with text and music attractive to children. It should also contain some definite musical feature (scale, phrase, or chord pattern) which is to be taught specifically through its use and which later will be stressed either in the study song or reading song. It may be a song already taught by rote provided it contains the features desired.

The **study song** is one which contains in addition to familiar phrases and tone groups, some new and unfamiliar groupings. Besides these it should have other characteristics useful in presenting facts of a technical or musical nature.

The **reading song,** sometimes designated as the "problem song" is one selected for reading and singing at sight. The first two or three songs selected for such purpose may be from those already learned by rote and used as observation songs. The next songs chosen should be new songs made up largely but not wholly of familiar phrases and tone groups. As the ability of the class to read and sing at sight increases, the characteristics of each new selection may be less and less familiar.

Procedure Leading to Sight Singing

Using the Observation Song. The first step in the rote-to-note procedure is through the observation song which should be used as follows:

1. Select an appropriate observation song, for example, *The Bells*[1]. First teach it by rote. Have the children express its pulsations by clapping or stepping the beats. Write the song on the blackboard and leave it there for a time so that each note may be pointed to as the children sing. Mark the direction of the melody on the blackboard, as shown on page 24, so that the eye may be trained to help the ear in determining the pitches. Children will gradually associate the position of the notes on the staff with the pitches, and also gain some understanding of note and rest values. This should be done before any direct explanation of the characters and symbols used in the notation of music has been attempted. Simply telling the children that music is written in such a manner will be sufficient in the beginning. The staff may be pictured to young children as a fence. The staff may also be effectively presented as a ladder with the leger line for Middle C as a short broken rung at the bottom.

---

[1] p. 116.

Melody Direction—*The Bells*

2. Sing the song for the pupils with the neutral syllable *loo*. Have the children identify the song. Then have them sing the song using the same syllable. While they are singing place long curved lines over the melody on the blackboard to indicate the phrases as illustrated.

Phrasing—*The Bells*

The children now sing the words of the song while the teacher numbers each phrase as it is sung. Individual children may next be asked to sing the song while a pupil points out the phrases. 3. Review the song by having the children sing it with the syllable *loo* and then with the words as the teacher again points out the phrases indicated on the blackboard. The phrases are now sung alternately with the syllable *loo*—the teacher singing a phrase, the pupils the next, and so on. Divide the class into two groups and have them sing the phrases alternately while a pupil points to the phrase marks on the blackboard. Lead the children to distinguish the phrases which are alike from those which are different. At this point the solfa syllables may be introduced and the pupils led to observe that like phrases have like syllables.

4. Before beginning the lesson write the song with its staff notation on the blackboard, omitting the time signature. Have the
children sing the words of the song while you mark on the blackboard the direction of the melody.

Compare these marks with the staff notation and show their
likeness in presenting the positions of the tones. The song is now
sung with the syllable *loo* while the teacher marks the duration
of its long and short tones, thus:

Duration of Tones—*The Bells*

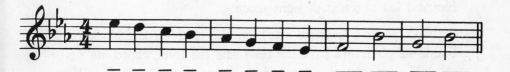

These duration marks are compared to the notes on the staff.
The class now claps, steps, or taps the rhythm or pulse to find the
number of beats in each measure. It is thus discovered that the long
tones require more beats than the short tones, that short tones
are represented by one set of characters (quarter-notes) and long
tones by another set (half and whole-notes). The quarter, half,
and whole-notes, and their equivalent rests may now be identified
and named. Separate the class into two groups. Have one group
count the number of beats in each measure while the other taps
the notes (one tap to each note). The teacher meanwhile points
to the notes on the staff. The pointer *must* be held on each note
for its proper duration. At this time various symbols and characters used in notation (staff, clef, key-signature, bar, measure)
may be named. The time signature is now placed on the blackboard and its meaning explained by application to the song. The
class again sings the words of the song while the teacher with
her pointer makes a curving motion over each phrase as it is sung.
The song is repeated using the sol-fa syllables, the teacher pointing the phrases as she did when the words were sung.

5. Sing to the class several phrases or tone groups with *loo* or the syllables and have the children locate them on the blackboard. As a test of the ability of the class to sing the song unaided have the children sing it with the syllables and then with *loo*. Parts that offer difficulties should be repeated two or three times, first with the syllables and then with *loo*. The song may then be sung with the words.

6. Review the song by having it sung with the syllables and then with *loo*. Write on the blackboard phrases and tone groups from songs previously learned by rote but which have not yet been used as observation songs. Have the class sing these with syllables and *loo* as a test of sight reading.

7. Next place a keynote (*do*) on the staff on the blackboard. Sound its pitch and have the class sing the tonic chord, *do - mi - sol*. The teacher or a pupil then writes it on the staff. Write several tone groups in different keys on the blackboard and drill on their recognition by singing them with *loo*. Flash cards may be used. These provide quick comparison of the same tone groups in different keys.

Several songs should be taught according to the foregoing procedure and each one learned should be reviewed frequently for the mere enjoyment of singing it.

Experience has proved that it is best to have three or four weeks of daily work with notation through observation song procedure before song-books are introduced. Pupils will then gain the ability to follow the smaller notation in the books as readily as they followed the larger notation on the blackboard. When they are able to do this they are ready for the Study Song.

Using the Study Song. This next step in the rote-to-note procedure is the use of a song containing some new and unfamiliar phrases and tone groups and providing a means of acquiring further technical knowledge of music. The first songs used for study purposes may be selected from those already learned by rote, but as the knowledge and ability of the class increases the proportion of unfamiliar material in the songs chosen should become greater. The following procedure for the use of the study song has been found effective:

1. Have the class examine the notation of a song to discover its familiar phrases and tone groups.
2. Have the class sing these familiar parts, first with the sol-fa syllables and then with the words.
3. Have the class discover an unfamiliar part in the song. This should be sung by the teacher and then by the class.
4. Have the class sing the song one phrase at a time, and then as a whole without interruption.

Many songs should be presented according to the foregoing procedure.

Usually the first study song is written on the blackboard and studied without reference to the song books. The use of the blackboard helps to concentrate the attention of the pupils upon the points the teacher is demonstrating. After the first few songs are thus presented, the books should be used. The songs *My Little Pony*[2] and *Autumn Leaves Are Falling*[3] are excellent for study purposes.

Using the Reading Song. The song chosen for reading at sight should be taught as follows:

1. Have the class examine the new song to discover its mood—whether lively or slow, sad or gay.
2. Let the children read and discuss the words that the meaning of the song may be understood.
3. Have the children discover familiar phrases or tone groups in the song and decide the character of the melody—whether it skips or is smooth and whether the rhythm is new or familiar.
4. Have the class sing the song with the neutral syllable *loo*.
5. Have the song repeated using the sol-fa syllables.
6. Have the class sing the entire song using the words. Give assistance only where needed.
7. Have the children sing new but simple songs from their books. Two splendid reading songs are *In September*[4] and *The First Snow*[5].

Develop accuracy and independent reading by requiring the pupils to follow the notation in the books closely. Watch the accuracy with which

[2]p. 110, [3]p. 108, [4]p. 101, [5]p. 120.

the children point out the notes as they sing them. If a child is not pointing accurately it is evident he is not reading independently but is merely
following the other children.

General Suggestions. The manner of starting a song for classroom work
is most important. To begin aright the following must be established: the
pitch of the keynote (do); a correct sense of the tonal relationships of the
key; the proper tempo; the correct beat of the measure upon which the
song starts. To realize these essentials the following procedure is recommended:

1. Sound the keynote on a pitch pipe or other instrument.

2. Have the class respond by singing do to the pitch given.

3. Have the class sing the tonic chord, do - mi - sol.

4. Have the class sing from do to the starting tone of the song
(in scale order).

5. Count two measures of the song in order to fix the tempo.
If the time signature is $\frac{4}{4}$ and the song begins on the primary or
first beat of a measure count the two measures in this fashion:
1, 2, 3, 4, 1, 2, 3, sing. If it starts on a weak or unaccented
beat, count 1, 2, 3, 4, 1, sing; or 1, 2, 3, 4, 1, 2, sing.

Insist upon a good independent attack that the children may be encouraged to have the confidence in their ability to make the correct start. Teach
them to follow the directing closely.

CHAPTER V

Part Singing

PART SINGING should not be undertaken until the children have learned to use their voices fairly well and considerable ability has been acquired in note reading and independent singing. The singers need to be trained to maintain the absolute independence of each part regardless of the movement of the others and to secure the proper blending so that both the melody and the supporting harmony stand out clearly. Loud singing or singing with forced tones should be guarded against. Keep the tones subdued enough so that the singers in each part may easily hear the others.

The following procedure will prove helpful in introducing part singing:

1. Teach a simple round by rote as a unison song. When the class is thoroughly familiar with it, have them sing it as a round. Call attention to the harmony resulting from the combined melodies.

2. Divide the class into two groups. Have one group sing the scale—*do, re, mi, fa, sol, la, ti, do*—while the other at the same time begins with *mi* and sings the scale—*mi, fa, sol, la, ti, do, re, mi.* Again call attention to the harmonic effect.

3. Divide the class into three groups and have them sing a triad. Begin by sounding *do* and have the first group take it up immediately and sustain it while the second group takes up and sustains *mi* and then the third group *sol* until the sign of release is given. Then give the signal for each group to sing its pitch simultaneously with the others, thus repeating the complete chord harmonically. Repeat this procedure with other positions of the same chord and in other keys. Alternate the parts, giving each pupil an opportunity to sing the different parts.

When the pupils are able to hold the pitch assigned to them against the other voices they are ready to sing simple two-part melodies, such, for example, as *Lightly Row*[1] and *All the Birds Are Here Again*[2]. As more and more independence and skill is acquired new selections of increased difficulty should be given. *Brahms' Cradle Song*[3] illustrates this second order of difficulty. When a number of such selections can be performed satisfactorily, three-part songs may be given such as *The Mountain Herd-Boy's Song*[4], *Down in the Valley*[5], and *Blow the Man Down*[6].

With unchanged voices it is advisable to alternate the parts, but the change should not be made on the same song. Until the pupils' voices begin to change, they should be able to go from one part to another freely and easily.

In selecting songs for the early work in part singing the harmonic aspects of the piece should be especially considered because the development of a feeling for harmony is an important objective in teaching part singing.

Since a fine blending of the voices is the ideal to be obtained, pupils should be directed to listen carefully to the harmony. Make each pupil realize his personal responsibility that every endeavor may be made to achieve expressive and accurate singing and the high degree of unity which is so much desired.

When any number of the class have manifested an ability to improvise it will prove interesting to have them devise appropriate parts while another group sings the melody of a song. It frequently happens in a class that much unsuspected talent for improvisation is uncovered and developed through an early experience with part singing.

---

[1]No. 83, The Silver Book of Songs—Victor Record 24241, [2]p. 126, [3]No. 82, S.B.—V.R. 20737, [4]No. 115, S.B., [5]p. 130, [6]p. 132.

CHAPTER VI

Rhythm

THE DEVELOPMENT of the child's rhythmic sense should go hand in hand with singing and play activities connected with school work. In securing the necessary physiological response to pulsations the teacher will do well to begin by having the children clap their hands, walk, skip, or run to the accompaniment of music, also by repeating nursery rhymes with or without the melody.

At first the child's response to rhythmic impulses may be awkward and far from accurate, due largely to difficulties in controlling and co-ordinating the motor centers involved. These troubles will soon vanish as the work is continued. As the child gains in ability to listen and the motor reflexes become more spontaneous, his motions will more and more accurately express the rhythmic pattern of the music, and he will be able to make intelligent and rapid adjustments to changes in tempo and expression. When responsiveness has been developed to some degree he is ready for such directed activities as marching, skipping, and stopping at musical command and taking part in singing games and folk dances.

Activities for the development of rhythmic consciousness and its expression may be classified as follows: free (interpretative), imitative, creative, and formal or directed.

Free Rhythmic Expression. Free rhythmic expression is the natural and therefore the simplest and easiest step for small children. The teacher begins by explaining that the motion (rhythm) and character of the music tells us something just as truly as words do. Because of their inexperience children are unable to sense this aspect of music until they are told that it is there. The skill with which the teacher presents this idea and her success in stimulating the imagination of the child will go far toward bringing out the desired free rhythmic expression. How one teacher effectively presented this idea to a class in the second grade is set forth in the following story of her procedure:

The phonograph record *The Teddy Bears' Picnic*[1] was used.

The teacher told the children that music tells a story or suggests

---

[1]Columbia Record 2720D.

something that may be done such as marching, dancing, swinging, or perhaps just going to sleep. She explained that she was
going to play a record and wanted the children to listen to the
music and then to do whatever it told them to do. If it told them
to dance, they were to dance. If it told them to march, they were
to march. If it told them to go to sleep, they were to lay their
heads on their desks and pretend to go to sleep. The expression
on the faces of the children showed that this opportunity to act
freely was a surprise to them and perhaps to be doubted a little
as to its reality.

The record was then played, but no explanation as to the character of the music was given. The children sat quietly listening
until about one-third of the record had been played. Suddenly a
little boy dropped to the floor on his hands and knees, but looked
doubtfully at the teacher. Being reassured by her expression that
he was at liberty to proceed, he started around the room on all
fours, growling like a bear; and soon three or four other children
followed, doing the same thing.

Of a Tailor and a Bear[2] by McDowell may be used in a similar
manner.

At first, in free expression the movements and attitudes of the children
are not very true to the character of the music. They are often crude and
wide of the mark, but as more attentive listening and a freer imaginative
response is developed the results of this practice become more satisfactory.

Imitative and Creative Rhythmic Expression. The observer of nature
will find many activities suggested for imitative rhythmic expression.
Rhythm Medley, Nos. 1 and 2[3] is recommended. In this record the sway-
ing of trees, the bending of grasses, the nodding of flowers, the heavy tread
of elephants, the trotting and running of horses, and the familiar motions
of birds in the air are all suggested.

The teacher should also lead the children to recognize and interpret in
their own way other rhythmic motions and sounds of familiar things and
activities—the chug-chug of a locomotive, the movements of pumping, the
swing of a pendulum, running without forward movement, et cetera. Chil-

2Victor Record 20153. 3V.R. 20526.

dren enjoy doing these things and quickly learn to interpret various rhythms.

Formal or Directed Rhythmic Activities. These are commonly expressed in singing games and folk dances. The singing game is, as a rule, the simplest of these and is therefore the most useful in teaching younger children directed movements, while the folk dance is better adapted to older children.

SINGING GAMES AND DANCES

I See You[4]. This selection is of Swedish origin. It is both a folk dance and a singing game. It is sometimes called the "Peek-a-boo" game and is useful in developing a feeling for the accent in $\frac{2}{4}$ measure.

Procedure

1. The children are divided into two equal groups. In one group each child is given the number 1. In the other group each child is given the number 2. The No. 1's form in two equal lines facing each other, about eight feet apart. They stand with hands on hips, spaced so that they will not touch elbows while in this position. The No. 2's stand directly behind No. 1's. Each No. 2 places his hands on the shoulders of the No. 1 in front of him.

2. All the children sing measures 1 to 4: "I see you, I see you, Tra, la, la, la, la, la, la, la, la".

3. On the first *see* No. 2's look over right shoulders of No. 1's.

4. On the second *see* No. 2's look over the left shoulders of No. 1's.

5. On the *Tra* No. 2's look over right shoulders of No. 1's.

6. On the sixth *la* No. 2's look over the left shoulders of No. 1's.

7. The same activity is continued during the singing of measures 5 to 8.

8. This section of eight measures is then repeated.

9. Singing continues through measures 9 to 12: "If I see you and you see me, Then I take you and you take me". On the word *If* all the No. 2's skip forward from behind the No. 1's, each No. 2 passing his No. 1 partner on the right. Each couple

4p. 102.

of No. 2's then join hands and whirl around once to the right.
A slide step may be used (two slides to the measure) instead of
the skip.

10. During the singing of measures 13 to 16: "If you see me and
I see you, Then you take me and I take you", No. 2's drop hands,
turn, and skip back to in front of their No. 1 partners. They,
No. 2's and No. 1's, join hands and skip around to the music,
stopping with No. 1's behind No. 2's, just the reverse of their
original position.

11. Repeat the game, but this time with No. 1's in the back rows
instead of No. 2's.

This number, when used as a folk dance, makes an attractive one for a
public program. When using it as a folk dance with older boys and girls,
the partners may hook arms instead of joining hands, first right and then
left, circling with a hop-step as they sing. When presented as a folk dance
the dancers do not sing but there should be an instrumental accompaniment, either a phonograph, piano, or orchestra.

———————

Wind the Bobbin (*The Shoemaker's Dance*)[5]. This Danish folk dance,
or singing game, in $\frac{2}{4}$ measure is recorded as "The Shoemaker's Dance."
It is a happy, easy dance that children love.

Procedure

1. Two circles are formed, one within the other, the girls in the
outer circle facing the boys in the inner circle. During the singing of measures 1 and 2 all whirl their hands as though winding
a bobbin.

2. For measures 3 and 4, the winding motion is reversed.

3. For measures 5 and 6, the tips of the fingers of both hands are
placed together and then pulled apart as though waxing a thread.

4. For measures 7 and 8, one fist pounds the other as though
hammering a tack.

5. The eight measures are repeated with the same motions; then
the singing continues through measures 9 to 12.

6. For measures 9 to 12, each boy clasps the hands of the girl opposite him. The pair then gallops four steps to the boy's left. The gallop is a lively sidewise hop.

7. For measures 13 to 16, the partners gallop back to place.

8. Repeat measures 9 to 16. At 16 partners change places by the girl moving forward to the next boy to the right.

9. For measures 17 to 24 repeat actions of measures 1 to 8.

The Mulberry Bush[6]. This is one of the better known singing games. It is useful in developing a feeling for the accent in $\frac{6}{8}$ measure.

Procedure

Children join hands and skip around in a circle as they sing the first stanza. During the singing of the other stanzas they stand and go through the motions suggested by the words. At the end of each stanza, on the words "So early in the morning" the children raise their hands, touch the tips of their fingers high above their heads forming an arch, and then turn around rapidly in their places.

A-Hunting We Will Go[7]. This old English singing game is useful for developing a feeling for the accent in $\frac{2}{2}$ measure.

Procedure

1. Children are arranged in two lines facing each other, boys in one line and girls in the other.

2. On the words "A-hunting we will go, A-hunting we will go" the first boy and first girl join hands and together they skip down between the two lines.

3. On the words "We'll catch a little fox, And put him in a box, And then we'll let him go", the couple drop hands, face about, clasp hands again, and skip back to their places.

4. The song is repeated, but this time all of the couples join hands and skip around in a circle with the first couple leading. When they complete the circle the first couple, with raised hands joined, form an arch. The next couple leads under the arch and

6p. 105, 7p. 107.

are followed by all the other couples. As each couple passes under the arch they separate and form into lines as they were in the beginning. This places the boy and girl that were second at the head of the new lines. The game is then repeated until all have been leaders.

5. For small children this game may be modified by having them form two circles. The inner circle clasps hands to form the box. The outer circle represents the hunters. One child is chosen to be the "fox" and runs lightly around the outer circle. At the word *go* in the song the child in the outer circle nearest the "fox" chases the fox and when he is captured puts him in the box. The fun of the game is caused by the uncertainty as to who will be indicated to catch the fox.

The game may be repeated until several "foxes" have been cap-tured and put in the box.

Jolly Is the Miller[8]. This is an old English singing game. It is useful in developing the feeling of accent in $\frac{4}{4}$ measure.

Procedure

1. Couples form a double circle with girls on the outside at the right of the boys. One of the boys is chosen to be the miller. Joining inside hands with their partners the couples walk around the circle, keeping step with the music as they sing. The miller stands in the center of the circle.

2. On the words "The lady steps forward and the man steps back", partners are changed. The miller tries to get a partner during the change. The one who is left without a partner becomes the miller and takes his place in the center. The game is then repeated.

ACCENT AND MEASURE

As in poetry, music is given symmetry and character by being organized according to regularly recurring groups of pulsations, and like poetry, the degree of stress given to the points of accent is a matter of interpretation and feeling. The first beat or point of accent in each group (measure)

always is given a more or less pronounced stress while the others are lightly
accented or are unaccented. However, even when not expressed, each beat
should be clearly felt. If one has a good sense of the meter (poetical measure) in poetry the recognition of and feeling for measure in music should
not be difficult. The grouping of accents into measures is commonly called
the "time" of the music. In ordinary musical measure the beats are grouped
in one or the other of the following arrangements: (1) strong, weak;
(2) strong, weak, weak; (3) strong, weak, medium, weak. Special drill
is often necessary to develop and establish a sense of measure and accent.
A practical procedure follows:

To illustrate the two-beat measure to children, write on the blackboard:

Twin - kle, twin - kle, lit - tle star;

Read the words to the children, giving considerable stress to
the accented syllables. Underline them as you read, thus:

<u>Twin</u> - kle, <u>twin</u> - kle, <u>lit</u> - tle <u>star</u>;

Suggest that a bar be drawn in front of each accented syllable,
and have the pupils tell where the bar should be placed. The
response should be "Before *twin,* before *twin,* before *lit,* and
before *star.*" As the placement of the bars is indicated, draw
vertical lines as follows:

| <u>Twin</u> - kle, | <u>twin</u> - kle, | <u>lit</u> - tle | <u>star</u>;

The children will readily see that the count for each measure is:

Twin - kle,	twin - kle,	lit - tle	star;
1 - 2	1 - 2	1 - 2	1 - 2
strong—weak	strong—weak	strong—weak	strong—weak

To illustrate the three-beat measure, write on the blackboard:

| Pick - a - back, | pick - a - back, | ba - by goes | by

The perception of the fact that the meter or time of this quota-
tion is 1-2-3, 1-2-3, 1-2-3, 1-2-3, that the emphasis or accent is
always on the number one count, and that the measure is marked
by placing a bar before the accented syllable, may be secured by
following out the same procedure as used with "Twinkle, twin-
kle, little star."

NOTE VALUES

When children have developed a feeling for accents in measure groups they are ready to be taught something of the relative duration of the sounds represented by different kinds of notes. The usual order of procedure is: (1) Training in the recognition of long and short tones; (2) sensing the number of beats in each measure; (3) expressing note values by tapping or stepping.

The following illustration placed upon the blackboard may be used to train children in the knowledge of two kinds of notes and their relative values.

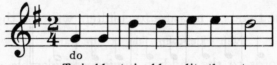

do
1. Twin-kle, twin-kle, lit-tle star;

The procedure for using the above illustration or a similar one is as follows:

1. Sing or play the phrase and tell the children to listen to the length of the tones. Have them locate the long tone.

2. As it is sung a second time, they listen to the accent and gently clap their hands to express the measure rhythm. The strong beat should be expressed by clapping the palms of the hands together—the weak beat by lightly tapping the palm of one hand with the finger tips of the other. This is important in getting the children to discriminate between strong and weak beats.

3. The rhythm having been established, the phrase is repeated while the children step (tap with foot) the notes lightly (a step for each note). They pause at the end of the phrase. Now play or sing the phrase again while the children listen for the strongly accented beats. Ask them how they would count the time. They should answer "1 - 2, 1 - 2, 1 - 2, 1 - 2."

The melody of *Twinkle, Twinkle, Little Star*[9] is available in record form under the title *The Question (Alphabet Song)*[10]. This is an excellent record for classroom use for it includes several selections excellent for illustrating two- and three-beat measures.

[9]p. 111, [10]Victor Record 22178.

Further Drill in Note Values. The following procedure for use with different kinds of measure presents further steps toward the establishment of a clear sense of note values and rhythms. If prior to this time the pupils have not incidentally or through specific instruction learned the identity of the whole-, half-, quarter-, and eighth-notes, the equivalent rests, and the dot, it will be advisable to explain and teach them before proceeding. The meaning of the time signature should also be explained in this connection.

1. The following exercise is to be written on the blackboard without the use of the staff.

The children's attention having been directed to the exercise, play it on a single pitch being careful to give each note its correct value. While this is being done the children indicate the duration of each note by tapping. The exercise is repeated with the children stepping each note. Then ask the pupils to identify the quarter-notes and the half-note.

2. The following exercise in ³ time is placed on the blackboard next to the preceding illustration so that the two may be seen in contrast. Proceed as in the previous exercise after explaining that a dot placed after a note increases its duration by one-half. Demonstrate how this applies to the half-note in the phrase.

3. Without erasing the two preceding phrases, write on the blackboard the following exercises which introduce the quarter-rest and the whole-note. Develop the fact that the quarter-rest is equal to the quarter-note. Follow the same procedure as before.

4. To introduce the eighth-note write the following on the black-board alongside the three preceding exercises and use the same procedure as before:

Devise other exercises as a means of presenting various note and rest values. For drill in learning note values the class may be divided into two groups. Then count the measure while one of the groups counts and beats the time with their arms, and the other lightly taps the note values on their desks. This practice is greatly enjoyed by children, but it should not be overdone.

EURHYTHMICS

The word eurhythmics is from the Greek, *eurhythmia,* meaning har-monious proportion or movement. In music it is now used in general to denote many simple physical expressions of rhythmic feeling such as tap-ping, hand clapping, marching, and various movements involved in singing games and interpretative dancing. Specifically the term refers to an elab-orate system of training evolved by Emile Jaques-Dalcroze for developing rhythmic feeling through harmonious and expressive bodily movements. The Dalcroze method aims at nothing less than the interpretation and expression of every aspect of music through the dance. The most elemental movements used to express rhythms such as tapping, walking, running, and skipping have already been mentioned. The Dalcroze manner of expressing beats and note values in walking is as follows:

For each *quarter*-note, a step.

For each *eighth*-note, a short quick trot-step, half as long in time as the walk-step for the quarter-note.

For each *half*-note (count of two), mark the count as follows: A walk-step on the first count, and a slight bending of the knee on the second count.

For each *whole*-note (count of four), mark the count as follows:
On the first count tap the floor with the right foot to the front.
On the second count tap the floor with the right foot to the side.
On the third count tap the floor with the right foot to the rear.
On the fourth count slide the right foot forward to its first position.

The song *America, the Beautiful*[11] is an excellent one for walking note values in $\frac{4}{4}$ time. Other phonograph records which will prove useful in this connection are:

Rhythm Medley, Nos. 1 and 2 (Victor Record No. 20526)
Fundamental Rhythms, Nos. 1 and 2 (V. R. 20350)
Fundamental Rhythms, Nos. 3 and 4 (V. R. 20351)
Rhythms for Children (V. R. 22168)

The following books will furnish interesting sidelights on the work of rhythmic developments:

Rhythms and Dances for Elementary Schools, Dorothy La Salle—A. S. Barnes & Co., New York
Rhythms of Childhood, Crawford and Fogg—A. S. Barnes & Co., New York
Rhythms for Home, Kindergarten, and Primary, Francis M. Arnold—Willis Music Co., Cincinnati

---

[11]p. 146.

CHAPTER VII

Song Dramatization

THE INTERPRETATION of a song by means of appropriate gestures or movements will employ to a greater extent the combined physical, mental, artistic, and social abilities of the child than any other single activity. Because song dramatizations are of the nature of play, they are of special interest to young children.

In directing song dramatization, see that the movements are gentle and graceful and never violent. If the song calls for energetic gestures, one group of the children may sing as another group dramatizes the song, or the entire class may participate in the dramatization while a phonograph plays the selection. A few selections and suggestions for their dramatization follow:

Autumn Leaves Are Falling[1]. The class stands and executes the following movements, suiting them to the words of the song.

First Stanza

1. Arms raised gracefully over head, then slowly lowered.
2. Repeat No. 1 movements.
3. Arms raised over head, then slowly lowered with rhythmic movement of the fingers to represent fluttering leaves.

Chorus

1. Rhythmic glide to right.
2. Rhythmic glide to left.
3. Repeat No. 1; then repeat No. 2.

Second Stanza

1. Arms upraised.
2. Arms slowly lowered with rhythmic fluttering of fingers.
3. Hands raised to mouth to imitate use of trumpet. Sing the word *trumpet* through the hands.
4. Arms upraised, fingers fluttering, as pupils revolve from left to right.

Chorus

Repeat as before.

----

[1]p. 108.

Third Stanza
1. Class stands with bodies relaxed, arms limp, and heads drooping.
2. Class sinks slowly to the floor, sinking into various free-play
positions according to their individual interpretations and inclina-
tions.
3. On floor, heads in drooping position with eyes closed, bodies
relaxed, voices gradually lowered to silence.
Chorus
Subdued humming of the melody.

The Grocer and the Housewife[2].   This musical conversation between a
grocer and a housewife, besides being a good number for dramatization, is
also useful for correction of out-of-tune singing. The boys act as the
grocer and the girls as the housewife. For individual work, a boy and girl
may sing the song as a duet.

Each pupil pretends he is using a telephone by placing his closed left
hand at his left ear and his closed right hand near his mouth. The girls
sing the first Hello; the boys the second. The girls order the bread, the
boys respond, and the girls sing the last Good-by.

Wind the Bobbin[3].   Besides being useful for dramatization, this selection is helpful in developing rhythmic feeling. The class may remain seated
during the singing.
1. While singing the words Wind, wind, wind the bobbin the
first time, the hands rapidly revolve around each other in imitation of winding thread. On the repetition of these words the
direction of the hands is reversed.
2. The tips of the fingers of both hands are placed together, and
on the word Pull, they are pulled in opposite directions as though
pulling a thread in sewing.
3. The right fist taps the left as if driving pegs with a hammer
while singing tap, tap, tap.
4. Motions 1, 2, and 3 are repeated.
5. The right hand is held aloft while singing Now we'll sew the

[2]p. 116, [3]p. 102.

right shoe O! and the left hand is raised while singing *Then we'll stitch the left just so.*

6. Movements of No. 5 are repeated.

7. Movements 1, 2, and 3 are repeated.

Bow, Wow, Wow[4]! For this selection the class stands and forms in couples. The action is as follows:

1. On the words *Bow, wow, wow!* hands are placed on the hips and the feet are stamped three times—right, left, right.

2. On *Whose dog art thou?* partners face each other, and with the elbows of their right arms in their left hands, point and shake their forefingers at each other to the time of the music.

3. On *Little Tommy Tinker's dog,* hands are placed on hips, and each pupil turns to the left and makes a complete circle in four short steps made to the rhythm of the music.

4. On *Bow, wow, wow!* the feet are stamped as in No. 1.

Jack-O'-Lantern Gay[5]. The action for this song is as follows:
First stanza

1. On the word *look,* children point and look toward a window.

2. On *awful thing,* each child leans away from the window and raises his hands in front of him as though frightened.

Second Stanza

1. On the word *Something,* the children pretend to look through eyeglasses made by bringing the ends of their thumbs and fore-fingers together in the form of circles.

2. On *See,* a step backward is taken to express fear.

3. On *Oh, I know,* the backward step is recovered and relief is expressed by relaxation.

4. On *jack-o'-lantern gay,* hands are clapped lightly but gayly.

The Windmill[6]. The children stand back to back in couples. One child raises his right arm to a little less than a perpendicular position and lowers his left to within a short distance of his body. The partner similarly raises his left arm and lowers his right. This gives the form of the windmill.

[4]p. 103, [5]p. 109, [6]p. 110.

1. On the first phrase of the song each child reverses the position of his arms by rhythmically dropping the upper arm as he raises the other with a slow sweeping motion.

2. On the second phrase the couples, keeping their backs together and arms in position, revolve to the right in time with the music.

3. On the third phrase, movement No. 1 is repeated.

4. On the fourth phrase, movement No. 2 is repeated.

Jolly Old St. Nicholas[7].   This song may be dramatized as follows:
First Stanza

1. On the words *Lean your ear this way,* the left hand is cupped back of the left ear.

2. On *Don't you tell a single soul,* pupils shake their right fore-fingers.

3. On *Whisper what,* both hands are cupped about the mouth as though whispering.

Second Stanza

1. On the words *When the clock,* a hand is extended toward schoolroom clock.

2. On *When I'm fast asleep,* palms of hands are placed together and left cheek is rested on them as though on a pillow.

3. On *Down the chimney broad,* arms are extended apart to indicate breadth of chimney.

4. On *With your pack,* both hands are raised to the left shoulder as though carrying a pack on the back.

5. On *Find the stockings,* a sweeping motion of the right hand is made toward fireplace (teacher's desk or some other designated object).

6. On *shortest one,* indicate length by holding hands a short distance apart.

Third Stanza

1. On the words *Nelly wants a picture book,* hands are held as though turning the pages of a book and looking at its pictures.

---

[7]p. 115.

2. On *Now I think*, forefinger of right hand is placed on right temple.

3. On *Choose for me*, a hand is placed on the chest.

Ten Little Indians[8]. This song is effectively dramatized by having the children appear one by one from outside the room or an imagined hiding place. As they sing the song, they walk around the room in Indian fashion until all ten little Indians have appeared. They then disappear in the same manner while singing the second stanza. The distance they walk should be such that the disappearance will begin with the beginning of the second stanza.

It will add much to the interest and attractiveness of this dramatization if the children wear head-bands which they can make for the occasion.

The Goblin Man[9]. This selection has unusual dramatic possibilities of which the following directions are but leading suggestions:

First Stanza

1. On singing the first *look out*, children jump back and turn away as though startled or frightened.

2. On the second *look out*, they look fearfully over their shoulders.

3. On *Goblin Town*, the children point with their right fore-fingers to an imaginary location of the town.

4. On *turn around*, the head is nodded to indicate they all agree that the goblin man will run away.

5. On *But oh my child*, the right forefinger is raised in the attitude of admonition or warning.

6. On the last two *look outs*, the head is shaken from side to side to give emphasis to the warning.

Second Stanza

1. On *creeps up*, children tiptoe forward with hands extended as if about to grasp someone.

[8]p. 112, [9]p. 164.

2. On first and second *look out*, head is turned from side to side as though looking to see that no one is behind.

3. On the third and fourth *look out*, the forefinger is held up and shaken to give emphasis to the warning.

4. On *You never know when he's around*, head is again turned from side to side to see if the goblin man is near.

5. On *now I've warned you*, the head is nodded and the forefinger shaken to give emphasis to the words.

6. On the last two *look outs*, emphasis is given to the warning by a more vigorous shaking of the forefinger.

CHAPTER VIII

The Rhythm Band

THE RHYTHM BAND or percussion band as it is often called, consists of a group of players of percussion instruments—that is, instruments that produce sound through being struck. In school work the special value of the rhythm band lies in its use with children as a means of creating and developing the rhythmic sense.

The rhythm band also has great educational value for the following reasons:

1. It provides an additional and interesting avenue of self-expression.
2. It is an aid in the development of concentration and musical discrimination.
3. It teaches the necessity and value of cooperation or teamwork.
4. It fosters independence, leadership, and general competence.
5. Through ensemble playing it results in greater enjoyment of music and a desire for further study.

Children from the ages of four to nine are usually chosen to form the band. The instruments used include rhythm sticks, drums, triangles, tambourines, cymbals, and others of like nature with or without the accompaniment of a piano or phonograph. All the players must produce sounds in accord with the rhythm of the music but not all instruments are played continuously throughout the performance.

A rhythm band may be formed as soon as the children manifest their ability to express accurately the simpler rhythms by clapping or stepping.

Because of the simplicity and cheapness of many of the instruments the formation of a rhythm band need not be foregone on account of expense. Rhythm sticks, rhythm blocks, tap bells, jingle bells, and triangles can easily be made or improvised. Frequently a successful demonstration of the use of these instruments makes funds available with which to purchase those which may not easily be made.

Beginners in the rhythm band first use the simplest of the percussion instruments such as rhythm sticks, triangles, and rhythm blocks. As the pupils gain the ability to use these, other instruments such as tone blocks, castanets, orchestra bells, and xylophones are added. In the beginning it is advisable to rotate the instruments among the pupils, but later they should be distributed according to the individual ability of the performers.

Since the idea of playing in a band is a fascinating one to all children, even to those who would not otherwise manifest a keen interest in music, it will be well to mention the formation of the rhythm band in connection with the first use of the rhythm sticks. Explain that as soon as these instruments can be used satisfactorily, the drum and other instruments as may become available will be introduced. As each new instrument is presented to the class it should be identified with its name and the manner of using it demonstrated.

Preparatory Step. As preparation for the introduction of the rhythm band, the following procedure is suggested:

Divide the class into two groups.

Have one group recite rhythmically the Mother Goose rime "Baa, Baa, Black Sheep", while the other recites in unison with the first group the triplet rhythm "Hey-diddle diddle the cat and the fiddle", stressing the first syllable of each triplet as shown by the following diagram:

A Baa	baa	black	sheep
1———————	1———————	1———————	1———————
B Hey did - dle	did - dle the	cat and the	fid - dle—
1 2 3	1 2 3	1 2 3	1 2 3

Before doing this exercise each group should practice separately its own rime, keeping strict count, until assured of being able to maintain the rhythm without confusion when the rimes are joined.

When the two groups have caught the idea of thus contrasting rhythms they may practice the rhythms by clapping their hands for each beat, group one clapping once while group two claps three times. Group two will show the accented beats with a little stronger clap.

Introducing the Rhythm Sticks. When the foregoing has been done successfully the idea of a rhythm band and its formation may then be presented and the rhythm sticks introduced and their use demonstrated. Each member of the class should then be given a set of rhythm sticks. Then as one of the groups recites a rhythmic selection, the other marks the rhythm and accent with their sticks. Next, the first group marks the rhythm and accent while the second group recites.

To carry the idea over into music, one group may sing a familiar song such as *Ten Little Indians*[1], while the other marks the beat and accent of the song with their sticks, or the entire class may mark the rhythm while the selection is being played on the phonograph or piano.

A further step in the initial use of the rhythm sticks is as follows:

1. Sing a familiar song such as *Twinkle, Twinkle, Little Star*[2], emphasizing very clearly the importance of the accent.

2. Then have one group of the class sing the selection while the other uses rhythm sticks to mark the beats.

3. Alternate the activities of the groups so that all may have an opportunity to use the sticks.

It is best for beginners to tap all the beats in each measure. Later when they have become more proficient they may tap every other beat (in measures of two or four). They will, eventually, be able to tap the first or accented beat in each measure only, counting the other beats to themselves.

Before adding other instruments to the band, the following use of the rhythm sticks is suggested:

1. Play on the phonograph *Fundamental Rhythms, No. 1*[3] and have the pupils listen for the accented beats of its rhythm.

2. Play the record again, having the children mark the accented beats with their sticks.

If all the children in the class have not been provided with sticks, those that do not have them may mark the accent by tapping on their desks with their fingers. If only a limited number of rhythm sticks are available, they should be passed from group to group so that all the children may have an opportunity to use them.

---

[1]p. 112, [2]p. 111, [3]Victor Record 20350.

Introducing the Drum. When the children are thoroughly familiar with the use of the rhythm sticks, the drum may be introduced. When the drum and rhythm sticks are used together, the former marks the accented beat, while the latter mark the weak beats. In the two illustrations which follow, the letter D stands for drum, and the letters RS for rhythm sticks. The teacher may count these exercises using the beat numbers, or she may play them on the piano while each instrument of the band takes its part. Beginners should count the beats in each measure throughout the entire exercise.

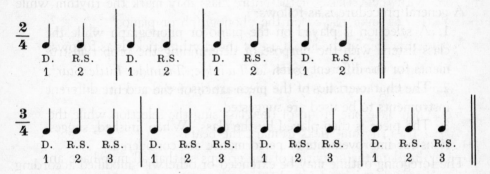

Exercises similar to the foregoing but in other varieties of time should be used until the class becomes proficient in marking their rhythms and accents.

Introducing Other Instruments. Having thus introduced the rhythm sticks and the drum, other instruments may be introduced progressively according to their difficulty in manipulation and the ability of the players to handle them successfully.

To facilitate the use of the instruments as a means of interpretation and expression a demonstration may be made showing how the instruments can suggest the sounds of creatures and things familiar through experience or through stories. For example, the sound of drums may be said to represent the growling of bears, the heavy tread of giants, the marching of soldiers, and the rolling of thunder. The tinkling of little bells may be used to express the fluttering of butterflies, the dancing of fairies, the rustling of leaves and other light and airy sounds. The jangle of the tambourine can be used to suggest the hurdy-gurdy man with his monkey, gypsy dances, and other tone pictures. Triangles may be used to represent the blows of a blacksmith's hammer on an anvil or any other thing having a similar metallic ring. The prolonged clash of cymbals may be used to represent the crash of thunder or the triumphant march of soldiers. These ideas should not be presented all at once but as the occasion for their use arises.

Developing Concentration and Discrimination. The rhythm band is a valuable help for developing concentration and musical discrimination. Through it use, children acquire the habit of listening attentively and interpreting what they hear.

A general procedure is as follows:

1. A selection is played on the piano or phonograph while the class listens with the purpose of determining the proper instruments for the different parts.

2. The characteristics of the piece are discussed and the different instruments to be used are suggested.

3. The piece is then played by the class. When finished, suggestions for improvements of performance are considered.

The foregoing outline may be extended or otherwise modified according to the musical knowledge and ability of the group. The procedure suggested not only offers the children an opportunity to express their own ideas and opinions, but it offers the teacher an opportunity to explain and present musical facts at a time when the children are really anxious to know them. The procedure involves a study of tonal effects which leads the pupils to discriminate between mere sound or noise and sounds having musical quality. By its use the pupils discover how certain instruments when played together tend to heighten the effect of each other. For example, the drum alone soon becomes monotonous. The rhythm sticks supplementing the drum vary and heighten the effect of the drum beat so that the combined effect is more enjoyable.

Furthermore, by means of a procedure such as the one suggested, pupils gradually begin to compare the sounds produced by two persons playing the same kind of instrument. They, therefore, learn to listen with discrimination and distinction for individual contributions to the ensemble as well as for the whole general effect.

Participation in the rhythm band, along the lines suggested, leads to an understanding of mood and to an ability to express it.

The Conductor.   Every child in the band should have an opportunity to conduct, no matter how limited his ability may be.   Giving every child an opportunity to lead helps to develop self-reliance and ofttimes discloses latent ability which might not otherwise be discovered.   For public performance, it is of course desirable to use the best conductor in the class. In practice beginners may lead by simply indicating the rhythm with movements of the hands.   When real ability to direct has been developed the pupil conductor may lead with a baton.

The ordinary requirement of a young conductor is that he mark the time, but where special ability is manifested the conventional gestures of a conductor for indicating the different measures may be taught.

Seating Arrangement.   The following diagram presents a generally accepted seating arrangement which provides satisfactory balance.   It may be modified to meet circumstances or conditions.

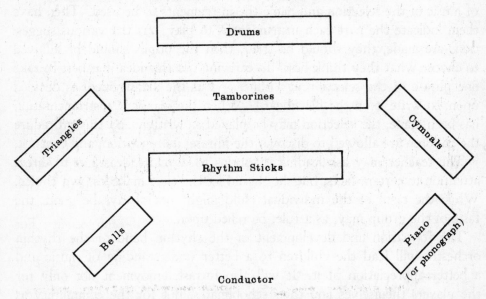

Whatever arrangement is selected it is well to have the players seated in the same order during practice as will be used for public appearance. By making this a rule, confusion and waste of time is avoided.   If the band is to appear on a stage, it is best to seat the players before the curtain is raised.   The effect on the audience of having players revealed to them as a unit instead of as a group of stragglers is electric and reacts on the players themselves in a very desirable and stimulating manner. This plan also helps to do away with nervousness among the players and avoids publicity of any confusion which may arise during the seating.

The Rhythm Orchestra. In some schools the rhythm band is developed into a rhythm orchestra, or toy symphony orchestra as it is sometimes called. The difference between a rhythm orchestra and a rhythm band is that the former uses in addition to the instruments of the rhythm band at least one instrument, besides the piano, having varied and variable pitch, such as the violin or the orchestra bells. The piano is used with both the rhythm band and the rhythm orchestra. Both the band and the orchestra should be closely correlated with the regular singing lessons. This correlation may be developed by having the pupils create the instrumentation of a familiar song such as *The Dancing Lesson*[4].

To develop the instrumentation have the children describe the type of music of the selection and name the instruments to be used. Then have them indicate the part each instrument is to play. As the various suggestions are made, they should be tried; then the pupils should be allowed to choose what they think best. In carrying out this idea it is best to take one phrase of the selection at a time, and as the arrangement is decided upon, to write it on the blackboard. When the complete instrumentation has been made, the selection may be played as written. By this procedure the children are allowed to discover the phrase, its repetition, and contrast.

The teacher may ask leading questions to develop ideas and to direct attention to certain facts, but she should let the class make its own choice. While the taste of the individual child might not always be good, the taste of the group may, as a rule, be relied upon.

The formation and development of the rhythm band or the rhythm orchestra will lead the children to a better understanding of music and a better appreciation of it. It will also furnish enjoyment not only for the players themselves and their schoolmates, but for the community as well. One should, however, guard against allowing the activity to become merely a display. The pupils should be led to see that the instruments must be played with precision and with the best tone quality possible, also that in order to produce the best results there must be perfect team work.

----
[4]p. 103.

Costuming the Band. It always adds to the attractiveness of the band
to have the children in uniform. A white cape and trench cap with a
bright colored band makes a simple but attractive combination that can be
made out of inexpensive material. For temporary use, they may be made
of crepe paper. If lack of funds or other circumstances make it impossible
to have uniforms, the band may be made attractive by having all the girls
wear white dresses with red ties, and the boys white blouses and red ties.

Other Readings. For additional information on the rhythm band and
orchestra, the following books are recommended:

Rhythm and Band Direction, Lyravine Votaw—Ludwig & Ludwig, Chicago.
The Toy Symphony Orchestra, Its Organization and Training, J. Lilian Vandervere—
C. C. Birchard & Company, Boston.
The Rhythm Band Series, Votaw, Luederash, and Mamheimer—The Raymond A.
Hoffman Company, Chicago.
Toy Symphony Orchestras, Irene St. Quentin—Oliver Ditson & Co., Boston.

CHAPTER IX

The Harmonica Band

THE HARMONICA BAND is a comparatively recent school activity. Some of the reasons why it has become a popular phase of school music are the limited amount of musical preparation necessary for good performance, the ease with which ear-minded children learn to play, and the low cost of the instrument itself.

The simplest procedure for organizing and building up a harmonica band is to start with those children who are able to play the instrument with some ability. The organization of such a group will stimulate other pupils with a desire to become members of the band. Some will learn to play by themselves, others will learn through instruction received from an experienced player, and still others will learn from instruction received from the teacher. As such pupils acquire ability to play independently, they should be added to the band. When organized, the group is drilled in playing with clear-cut melody and correct time and phrasing. In giving such instruction a violin or piano will be found helpful as a lead. Since the ordinary harmonica can be played only in one key the lead instrument must of course use that key.

For the benefit of those teachers who do not know how to play the harmonica and may have occasion to tell their pupils how to play it, the following instructions are condensed from Hohner's "The Art of Playing the Harmonica", a useful book available through any music dealer.

How to Play the Harmonica

Fundamentals. The harmonica is held in the left hand with the low or bass notes to the left. In playing, the mouth usually covers four holes. The instrument is placed well into the mouth between the teeth so that four holes are covered. The tongue is placed firmly against the three holes to the left, thus leaving but one open to be sounded by blowing or drawing the breath through it. To play the different notes the harmonica is moved back and forth across the mouth so as to bring the melody notes into the position just described.

To Play the Scale.   On the ordinary harmonica *do* is sounded by blowing through the fourth hole from the left.   *Re* is sounded by drawing the breath through the same hole.   *Mi* is sounded by blowing the breath through the fifth hole, and *fa* by drawing the breath through the same hole.   In like manner the other notes of the scale are sounded.   Beginners should practice much on sounding *do* and then on playing the scale before undertaking to play pieces.   The reeds in the holes above the seventh provide a continuation of the scale into the next octave.

Chord Effects.   The chord accompaniment to a melody is readily obtained by moving the tongue on and off the harmonica in rhythm with the melody.   This "tonguing" provides a simple three-note accompaniment. The solo note is continuously exposed to the breath.   The three holes that are covered by the tongue constitute the notes of the chord, and the tongue should be moved on or off of them as many times as there are counts to a measure.   Through this manipulation a harmonious effect is obtained, and it also helps to keep proper rhythm.

Vibrato Effects.   The tonal quality of the harmonica may be greatly enhanced through a manipulation of the hands over the instrument.   To secure the best quality and roundness of tone, the harmonica is held in the left hand between the index finger and thumb.   The thumb of the right hand is placed beneath the thumb of the left hand, and the fingers of the right hand are closed over those of the left, forming a box or air chamber.   With the hands in this position the right hand is opened and closed rapidly in such a way as to open and close the box or air chamber, thus producing an effective vibrato.

Notation for the Harmonica.   The numbers given in the notation written especially for the harmonica refer to the holes of the instrument as they run in rotation from left to right.   For example, the figure 1 refers to the first hole, 2 to the second hole, 3 to the third hole, and so on.   Although the letters B (for *blow*) and D (for *draw*) are used occasionally to indicate the direction of the breath in playing, the usual custom is to print the figure alone when the breath is to be blown, and to print an apostrophe after the figure when the breath is to be drawn.   For example, the figure 4 alone means to blow through the fourth hole.   The figure 4 with the apostrophe after it thus, 4', means that the breath is to be drawn through the fourth hole.

CHAPTER X

Music Appreciation

TRUE MUSIC APPRECIATION is not the mere enjoyment of music; it is much more. To the musician it signifies a fine discrimination in sensing differences in the qualities of tone; a sensitive understanding of the melodic, harmonic, rhythmic, and formal elements of music; a well developed musical memory; and an acquaintance with the masterpieces of musical art of all time. Thus music appreciation is that enjoyment which results from a cultivated understanding of all that pertains to the art.

In the school there are four important means of developing appreciation: by having the children participate in singing (and playing), with special attention paid to aural and rhythmic training; by development of the imagination and deepening of the emotional response to music; by instruction in the simple rudiments of music; and by correlating music with other studies, activities, and interests.

Participation in Singing. The chapters devoted to rote singing, sight singing, rhythm, and part singing provide the procedures for the first named means of developing appreciation. Through these activities a beginning is made in sensing melodic and harmonic successions and in feeling and responding to various rhythms.

Development of Imagination and Emotional Response. Developing the child's appreciation of music through cultivating his musical imagination and deepening his emotional response is greatly aided if the ideas and associations expressed in his songs are clearly brought out and elaborated. The power of music to suggest and express a wide range of emotions and ideas should be constantly illustrated to the children. For example, the musical and rhythmic features present in a lullaby brings a certain type of emotional response. Every piece of music taught to the child should be provided with a story or illustrated by some idea within his experience whereby an association may be established with his feeling and imagination. This need not be supplied by the teacher in every instance. Indeed it is much better for the child to express his own reactions in his own way while the teacher merely guides and corrects. All lesson material must be considered from the child's point of view. Children love a story, and music that tells a story which they understand makes a strong appeal to them.

Very useful in making the "story" approach to music appreciation are two phonograph recordings which present eight selections from Humperdinck's Opera *Hansel and Gretel*.[1] The lovely simplicity and beauty of the music and the charm of the story make it a masterpiece of particular attractiveness to children.

Other excellent records with story material for children are the following:

The Hunt in the Black Forest[2]. This record tells a story that children enjoy—especially boys.

1. Before playing the record the teacher tells the story of The Fox Hunt. In this is brought out the gathering of the men on their horses at the first cock crow and the exciting chase with the hounds which follow until the fox is caught. Sometimes a horse casts a shoe and the blacksmith has to reset it. The hunter's horn is sounded to call together the dogs and the riders.

2. The record is then played and the children listen. The record is played again. This time the children should be able to recognize the barking of the dogs, the galloping of the horses, the hunter's horn, and the blacksmith's hammer.

Narcissus[3]. This record provides another interesting story in music.

1. Tell the story of Narcissus. Make the story as graphic as possible, stressing certain parts such as the attractiveness of the boy, the changing of him into a flower, the reflection of his face in the water. Do not tell the children why these parts are stressed.

2. Play the record and let the class discover that the first part of the music which is attractive and pleasing describes the boy; he was attractive and pleasing so the music must express these characteristics.

3. Ask such questions as "Which part of the music describes the boy changing into a flower? Does any part of the music nod like a flower?"

---

[1]Victor Records 22175 and 22176, [2]V.R. 35792, [3]V.R. 21449.

4. Play the record a second time and lead the class to notice how each phrase is reflected by a similar phrase. In this way the music pictures the boy's face in the water.

Also show by the use of a natural or an artificial narcissus that the flower bends over as if it were seeing itself in the water. Tell the children that the narcissus always grows in moist places, usually along the edge of a brook or a pond. Through these ways of association, music and literature are related to something very concrete and familiar, and the result will probably be that every narcissus that the child sees will be associated with both literaure and music.

Nocturne (Midsummer Night's Dream)[4]. This Nocturne from Mendelssohn's suite is said to be a perfect melodic gem in a perfect harmonic setting.

The Nocturne may be taught in its vocal arrangement. The text is descriptive of the midnight air in the forest when the revelers from the village and the fairy folk as well have vanished and the forest sleeps in quietness and solitude. The children will be interested in analyzing the text in order to discover whether the music really expresses the mood of that exquisite tone picture. They may wish to dramatize this picture. It may be worked out as a school project.

Rudiments, Form, and Structure. The third important means of developing music appreciation is through a knowledge of the rudiments of music, its forms and structure. These have been treated in some detail in other chapters. The sense of form and structure really begins when the child is able to feel the tonic of a key as the "home-tone", the point of rest, and the only completely satisfactory tone upon which a composition may end. Simultaneously he feels the effect of cadence and half cadence without being able to define them. Since phrases customarily end in a cadence the first lessons in form should begin with the study of the phrase. The question and answer aspect of successive phrases should be fully brought out. Although the subject of phrases was touched upon in the section devoted to the observation song, the method to be followed will be treated more fully at this point.

[4]Victor Record 22765.

The old German melody *Twinkle, Twinkle, Little Star* may be used once more, for this purpose. There are six phrases of four measures each in the song. Phrases 1 and 2 are unlike and represent a question-answer relation.

The teacher sings or plays the first phrase once or twice; then the second phrase. The children should be told to listen for the difference between the two phrases. Arrange the class in two groups and have one group sing the first phrase, the other group following immediately with the second phrase, thus illustrating the question-answer effect. However, phrases may be exactly alike as in phrases 3 and 4. The teacher should sing these phrases.

Then have one group sing phrase 3 and the other group phrase 4 while the teacher emphasizes their identical form. The teacher next sings phrases 5 and 6.

Lead the class to observe that phrases 5 and 6 are repetitions of 1 and 2 and likewise that there are three parts to the song: (A), phrases 1 and 2; (B), phrases 3 and 4; (A2) phrases 5 and 6. Put the song in notation on the blackboard and also make a diagram of the parts and their relations as given below.

DIAGRAM

A	B	A2
phrases 1 and 2	phrases 3 and 4	phrases 5 and 6
		(Repetition of 1 and 2)

Carry out the above procedure with several other simple songs of your own selection.

Use the phonograph to teach simple instrumental two- and three-part forms and such types as the march, the waltz, and the minuet. As the pupils become better able to recognize song patterns and instrumental two- and three-part forms and as they more quickly sense various rhythms, their interest in and enjoyment of music will increase.

Correlation.   The fourth important means for the development of music appreciation is correlation.

The correlation of the folk music of our own and other lands with the social sciences is an important means for developing a sympathetic understanding of regional and racial traits and attitudes; and because it expresses the hopes, joys, and sorrows common to all humanity it is one of the most potent influences in eradicating racial prejudice and promoting a real sense of the brotherhood of man.

There is scarcely a phase of nature that has not served as the theme for a song or instrumental composition. These reflections of nature in tone intensify the impressions which a child receives from his daily experience and study. They deepen and refine his emotional response and broaden his culture and understanding.

The matter of correlating music with literature and art is relatively easy. Most of the lyrics of songs were first written as literature and subsequently set to music, because the rhythm and content of the poem prompted musical expression. Poetry and prose have also influenced the creation of many fine works purely instrumental in character. It has been proved that appreciation of pictorial art is greatly enhanced when associated with appropriate music. Sculpture, architecture, and even industrial arts can often be interpreted more effectively to students by means of songs and instrumental music. For children particularly such pictures as the "Song of the Lark" and "The Angelus" make a stronger appeal if suitable music is used when presenting them.

MATERIAL FOR CORRELATION

A vast amount of music on phonograph records and in school song books provides for every conceivable need for correlation in the development of music appreciation; therefore it will not be necessary to give here more than a few suggestions of available material and how to use it.

For correlation with rhythmic play there are cradle songs, boat songs, work songs, singing games, and folk dances. The chapter in this book devoted to Song Dramatization will be found helpful to teachers who feel the need of detailed suggestions for use of such material in school room games and exercises. Specific numbers which are especially useful in this connection are *The Bridge of Avignon*[5], and *The Dancing Lesson*[6]. These selections abound with rhythmic life and appropriate word imagery which makes them especially valuable in music appreciation work based upon play.

Songs expressive of man's feeling for nature are numerous. The heavenly bodies, seas, lakes and streams, the seasons, birds, and other animals have all been subjects of musical compositions. Many forms of vegetation have also been interpreted by means of tone. There is a very interesting and close relationship between the development of the musical composition from motive and phrase to its complete musical form, and the growth of a plant from seed to bloom. In both processes the operation of a rhythmic law is discernible, for there is a common rhythm of line, form, and color and a logical order in structure and design. Among the nature songs with a special appeal to children which may be used are the following: *The Telescope*[7], *The Cuckoo*[8], *The Robin*[9], *The Goldenrod is Waving*[10], and *Old March Wind*[11].

Means for correlating music and art are suggested by the following type lesson. The equipment necessary is a phonograph; the three instrumental records: *The March of the Tin Soldiers*[12], *The Elfin Dance*[13], and *Cradle Song (Brahms)*[14]; and a picture of "Madonna and Child". The procedure for the use of these is as follows:

The teacher explains that every picture and every piece of music has a story to tell. Through questions and answers the mood of the picture, "Madonna and Child", is developed. The teacher then plays the three records while the pupils listen attentively to them. When the playing is ended, the pupils are asked which record expresses the same thought as that expressed by the picture.

[5]p. 107, [6]p. 103, [7]No. 56, The Silver Book of Songs, [8]p. 113, [9]p. 117, [10]No. 41, S.B.—Victor Record 24539, [11]p. 109, [12]V.R. 20399, [13]V.R. 20079, [14]V.R. 20174.

The same procedure may be used associating the picture entitled "The Angelus" with *Now the Day Is Over*[15]. "The Song of the Lark" may be used with *When Morning Gilds the Skies*[16].

Another procedure which is just the reverse of the foregoing is to play a record and have the pupils choose from several pictures the one whose mood matches that of the music.

Many poems by Longfellow, Stevenson, Eugene Field and others which are attractive to children have been set to music. These afford splendid examples of the power of music to heighten the emotional and dramatic content of verse. For instance, the words of the song *Carillon*[17], written by Longfellow, describe his memories of a visit to the old Flemish town of Bruges with its famous bell tower in the market place. The study of such a song cannot fail to be inspirational. The lovely two-part setting of Stevenson's *Night and Day*[18] and the two-part setting of Wordsworth's *The Daffodils*[19] are also fine examples of the marvelous way music can enrich the expressive power of true poetry.

Another form of literature adapted for correlation which should not be neglected is that which deals with humorous characterization, description, and suggestion. Such literature has its counterpart in music, and the correlation of the two is of value. Some of the children's songs available for use in this connection are *Captain Hook*[20], *The Chinese Vegetable Man*[21], *The Sleepy Fishes*[22], and *A Frog He Would A-Wooing Go*[23]. For older students excerpts from light operas are useful. Modern orchestral literature also contains many notable compositions in which the element of humor finds abundant expression. Outstanding examples of these are *Till Eulenspiegel*[24] by Richard Strauss and *The Sorcerer's Apprentice*[25] by Paul Dukas.

The Symphony Orchestra*. An important and essential step in furthering the progress of students in appreciation is to teach them to identify by name and tone quality the instruments of the symphony orchestra. They should be taught the four choirs or sections into which the orchestra is divided and the instruments included in each section in the following

*For the teacher who wishes to give further attention to the instruments of the orchestra, the material called "The Instruments of the Orchestra by Sight, Sound, and Story," RCA Victor Company, Inc., Camden, New Jersey, is highly recommended.

[15]No. 155, The Silver Book of Songs—Victor Record 21936, [16]No. 169, S.B.—V.R. 22626, [17]No. 128, S.B.—V.R. 24541, [18]No. 77, S.B.—V.R. 22166, [19]No. 103, S.B.—V.R. 24540, [20]p. 104, [21]p. 118, [22]No. 43, S.B.—V.R. 24536, [23]p. 124, [24]V.R. 9271-9272, [25]V.R. 7021.

order: (a) the strings, (violin, viola, cello, double bass, and harp); (b) woodwinds, (piccolo, flute, clarinet, oboe, English horn, and bassoon); (c) brasses, (cornet, trumpet, trombone, French horn, and tuba); (d) percussion, (celesta, bells, chimes, xylophone, timpani, snare drum, bass drum, castanets, cymbals, triangles, and gongs). Other instruments such as the saxophone are sometimes called for in modern compositions.

The string, brass, and woodwind choirs are composed of instruments capable of playing melodies while the percusssion section is limited largely to purely rhythmic effects. Of this latter group the celesta, chimes, and xylophone are capable of sounding melodies but they are seldom used independently by composers for such purposes. They are usually employed with other melodic instruments to add color.

Because of the great variety in range and tone quality of the instruments in the string, woodwind, and brass sections, and the fact that each can produce within itself harmony in four or more parts, these choirs are used independently as well as in combination.

In familiarizing students with the tone quality of the separate instruments Victor Records Nos. 20522 and 20523 will be found especially valuable. Accompanying the demonstration of each instrument a picture of it should be displayed where all may see it. Frequent repetition of these records should be made. Tests should also be made of the ability of each member of the class to name the instruments from sound alone.

SOURCE MATERIAL FOR MUSIC APPRECIATION

In conducting her classes the teacher should endeavor to stimulate the interest of students by giving them information suited to their years regarding the history of music and the lives of composers. When mentioning the name or music of a master the teacher is advised to present at the same time some relevant facts which have to do with his life, the period in which he lived, or his important compositions. For younger children stories and anecdotes are especially valuable. From a long list of excellent books containing material suitable for children of all ages, the author recommends that the following be consulted:

Music Stories for Girls and Boys, Donzella Cross—Ginn & Company, Boston.
What We Hear in Music, Anne Shaw Faulkner—RCA Victor Co., Inc., Camden, N. J.

Music and Romance, Hazel Gertrude Kinscella—RCA Victor Co., Inc., Camden, N. J.

Listening Lessons in Music, Agnes Moore Fryberger—Silver, Burdett & Company, New York.

Music Appreciation Readers, Hazel Gertrude Kinscella—University Publishing Company, Chicago.

The Listeners' Guide to Music, Percy Scholes—Oxford University Press, New York.

Lessons in Music Understanding, Kathryn Stone—Southern California Music Co., Los Angeles.

Instruments of the Orchestra Hand Book, RCA Victor Co., Inc., Camden, N. J.

Music Appreciation with the Victrola for Children, RCA Victor Co., Inc., Camden, N. J.

Music Appreciation, Clarence G. Hamilton—Oliver Ditson Company, Boston.

Music to the Listening Ear, Dr. Will Earhart—M. Witmark & Sons, New York.

Discovering Music, Howard D. McKinney and W. R. Anderson—American Book Company, New York.

Listening To Music, Douglas Moore—W. W. Norton & Company, New York.

The Education of a Music Lover, Edward Dickinson—Charles Scribner's Sons, New York.

CHAPTER XI

Creative Music

CREATIVE ability in the field of music can be developed in children if they are encouraged and taught to practice the composition of little melodies. The talent for writing couplets and quatrains is fairly common among children. When present in a child, this talent is an evidence of a certain fortunate combination of gifts that are much the same as those required for creative work in music. These gifts include a sensitive imagination, a feeling for rhythm and symmetry, a sense of word color, and the ability to make effective associations and contrasts in ideas. If the teacher possesses a reasonable degree of skill, enthusiasm, and patience, the composition of little songs will become a perfectly natural play activity from which the child will derive the greatest pleasure and benefit. If these creative processes are to come to their proper development, considerable latitude must be allowed that the spontaneous reactions of the child may be given full expression. The songs he already knows will naturally influence the form and direction of his musical thought. True growth, however, comes from free experiment. Such impulses on the part of the child should receive instant encouragement.

The first exercises with younger children should consist of simple question and answer songs between teacher and pupil using the tones of the tonic chord. They should not be more than four measures in length—two measures for the question, and two for the answer. Pupils will quickly grasp the nature of these exercises and manifest pleasure and interest in them.

The teacher sings the question, "What shall we sing?" using the tones 1, 3, 5, 8 (do, mi, sol, do). The child may reply, "The Bluebird Song" or some other appropriate answer using either the tones 8, 5, 3, 1 (do, sol, mi, do), or a series of his own choice. Other simple question and answer songs such as "Where is the bird?", "Up in the tree," and "Who has the ball?" "I have the ball" can be devised to fit the following note arrangements:

(question) 1, 3, 1, 5 (do, mi, do, sol)? (answer) 5, 3, 5, 1 (sol, mi, sol, do).

(question) 3, 1, 3, 5 (*mi, do, mi, sol*)? (answer) 3, 5, 3, 1 (*mi, sol, mi, do*).
(question) 5, 3, 5, 8 (*sol, mi, sol, do*)? (answer) 8, 3, 5, 1 (*do, mi, sol, do*).

With the gradual addition of other tones from the scale series, the songs become much more various and interesting. The teacher need only offer occasional suggestions and corrections to the children. It should never be forgotten that the sense of the *rightness* of the tone relations existent in the major scale is instinctive, and therefore neither argument nor tedious repetition is necessary in training students to feel the tonic as the parent tone and the center of attraction.

The following are other examples of note arrangements for question and answer songs:

(question) 1, 3, 4, 5 (*do, mi, fa, sol*)? (answer) 5, 4, 2, 1 (*sol, fa, re, do*).
(question) 1, 2, 4, 3 (*do, re, fa, mi*)? (answer) 5, 2, 3, 1 (*sol, re, mi, do*).
(question) 5, 3, 6, 5 (*sol, mi, la, sol*)? (answer) 4, 2, 5, 1 (*fa, re, sol, do*).
(question) 5, 7, 8, 6 (*sol, ti, do, la*)? (answer) 5, 6, 7, 8 (*sol, la, ti, do*).

A Lesson in Creative Music. As the work progresses melodies may be composed to couplets which the children themselves should be urged to write, or they may be taken from other sources. In either case the metrical form of the verse will need to be such that only simple note values are required for its expression. The following is a good example of a suitable couplet as regards both meter and word content:

> Hear the merry, merry rain
> As it taps the window pane.

Having written or printed it on the blackboard the teacher reads the couplet to the class and then gives the children an opportunity to express their thoughts and feelings regarding rain and why it may be spoken of as "merry". They may also be questioned as to the kind of music which would best express the poem—a tune that is slow or one that is gay and dancing.

The class reads the couplet aloud rhythmically, tapping the beats lightly while the teacher marks the accents using straight lines for principal accents and curved lines for secondary, and places bar lines as follows:

Hear the	mer · ry	mer · ry	rain,
As it	taps the	win · dow	pane.

The measure divisions and the principal and secondary accents having been made clear, the teacher asks if any child has a tune for the first line. Let several of the children sing their tunes and the members of the class decide which one they like best. In assisting the children to make a choice and in developing reasons why this or that melody is to be preferred, the teacher should lay emphasis on any original features it may possess. Repeat the new melody until all are familiar with its general outlines.

The tune for the first line having been selected, its rhythmic structure is pictured on the blackboard thus:

The class will now indicate the strong and weak beats by clapping, giving a stronger clap on the principal accents, while the teacher puts the accent marks above the notes thus:

Again have the pupils indicate the accents by tapping on their desks.

They are now prepared to sing the melody with the neutral syllable *loo* after which the teacher places the sol-fa syllables on the blackboard beneath the notes as shown by the example below. The song is then repeated using these syllables.

sol   mi   sol   mi   re   re   mi

The second line of the couplet is read and the children asked to supply a melody for it. Follow exactly the same procedure as was given for developing the first line of the verse. When all the details of preparation have been completed have the class sing the entire song using the syllables.

The next step to be taken is the writing of the melody on the staff. After discussing the question of which key would be best, the teacher, wishing to keep the range well within the staff, will lead the children to chose E or F possibly as the proper key. A decision on this point can be easily arrived at by having the class sing the song in three or four different keys, one of which will quite evidently be best suited to their voices. The teacher now places the clef and key signature on the staff.

In order to establish a clear sense of the total relations in the key selected, the teacher sounds *do* and has the children sing the tones of the tonic chord (*do-mi-sol*) in succession. As they are sung the teacher writes them on the staff with their syllable names and then as a chord as shown by the following example.

Having thus fixed the tonality in their minds the class is asked to give the syllable names of the notes of the melody composed for the couplet and to give their correct position on the staff. As the place of each note is determined the teacher writes it on the staff. The notation completed, the pupils clap or tap the rhythm of the music so as to decide where the bars separating the measures are to be placed and what the time signature is to be. When these have been determined and written on the staff, the words of the song are put beneath the notes and the song sung by the class as written. Individual students may also sing the selection or play it on the piano. The following illustration shows the song as it might appear when completed.

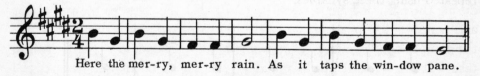

Here the mer-ry, mer-ry rain. As it taps the win-dow pane.

The working out of an accompaniment for a song of the type given would be of great interest and value to the class. In this instance the tonic and dominant or dominant seventh chords, are sufficient to provide an adequate harmonic background. If possible lead the pupils to choose the most satisfactory from several suggested accompaniments and help them to discover reasons for their choice. They might be told that the chord best suited to accompany a given part of a melody is always the one with which it has the most notes in common. Thus measures one,

two, four, and five, six, eight of the illustration contain tones belonging
in the tonic chord while measures three and seven contain tones belonging
to the dominant and dominant seventh chords of the key. Call the tonic
triad the *do* chord and the dominant triad the *sol* chord. Other chords
can be identified in like manner when met with. The accompaniment for
the song when worked out should be placed on the blackboard on a staff
below the melody staff in the manner illustrated below.

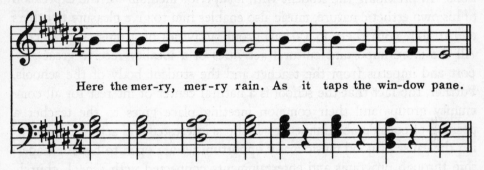

Here the mer-ry, mer-ry rain. As   it   taps the win-dow pane.

If rests are used as in the preceding illustration, the reason for their
use should be explained and their relative time-values demonstrated. In
a case similar to the present instance, children would easily understand how
the use of quarter-notes in the accompaniment for measures five, six, and
seven helped to express the idea of the rain tapping on the window.

Encourage the pupils to compose melodies, outside of school hours, for
any rimes that may appeal to their fancy, and if they are able to do so,
let them copy their songs on the blackboard and sing them to the class
during the music period. It will be found that the sense of phrase-balance
and contrast developed in the work with couplets makes the next step—
the composition of music to fit a quatrain—a comparatively easy one to
take. The stimulus to the imagination, the quickened rhythmic sense, and
the practical experience with different note and rest values gained from
this creative work gives it great educational utility.

A word should be said about the choice of rimes. The more various
in rhythm and imagery the couplets or quatrains chosen for use in the
class may be, the better. This will make possible a wide range of musical
experience for the children. The "Mother Goose" rimes and almost any
school edition of children's poems will provide material adapted for use
in this connection.

CHAPTER XII

School Music and the Community

THE STUDY and practice of music while essentially a matter of self-expression and culture, possesses great value to the individual in his social relations. In providing the student with a superior medium for the expression of his own esthetic nature, music also enables him to give pleasure to others and to join with them in various group activities of a musical character. All the more important cultural activities of a locality receive great support and impetus from the teacher and the student body of the schools. Further, the fact that the school is a natural center of interest for all community groups and their common meeting place gives to the teacher a position of considerable influence. If she is interested and active in promoting the cause of good music many opportunities are open to her for leadership through programs and entertainments connected with school, church, and other community gatherings.

If a school choir or chorus has been developed it may be used in local programs not only as a means of providing special entertainment but in order to demonstrate the value to the community of the music study pursued in the schools. Care taken in the selection and rehearsal of the programs given on these occasions will cause a very important increase in enthusiasm and appreciation on the part of students, parents, and the community at large. A success in this field is certain to add to the prestige of the teacher and to create a legitimate pride in the hearts of the people in her achievement.

Community music need not be restricted to group singing. Instrumentalists and singers of ability from among the students should be asked to contribute solo numbers and local church choirs, bands, and orchestras, may also take part.

In directing the performance and rehearsal of programs and particularly of community singing the services of a really competent accompanist at the piano will be of great assistance to the teacher. If she is unable to secure such help phonograph recordings of bands or orchestras playing standard song accompaniments will prove satisfactory. The songs selected for singing at community affairs must of necessity be such as are widely known and appealing to the mass of people. These are most often patriotic and national airs of the folk song type but popular songs of the day may also be used if they are free from vulgarity both in text and music.

Besides the programs mentioned and the music for special holidays, a suitable observance of Music Week, the first week in May, will help to create a wider appreciation and enjoyment of music. Whenever possible the effort should be made to secure the active cooperation of all churches, lodges, clubs and similar organizations in preparing special programs of their own. Such a local festival week could well begin stressing the part of music in church services. On successive days the lodges, the clubs, and the schools could give programs. An afternoon devoted to singing games, folk dances, physical education exercises, the performance of an operetta, and a band or orchestra concert are appropriate features which are sure to arouse interest and enthusiasm.

Additional information and suggestions may be found in *Music in American Life* by Augustus D. Zanzig, published by American Recreation Association, New York. A suitable school and community song book is *The New American Song Book*, published by Hall & McCreary Company, Chicago.

CHAPTER XIII

Rural School Music

THE NEED for music is, on the whole, greater in rural schools than in those of the towns and cities because the opportunities for coming into direct contact with musical activities and participation in them is often quite limited. This is not only true of music but of all cultural influences. The automobile and the vast improvement in highways during the past years have made access to concerts, lectures, exhibitions and the like in towns and cities comparatively easy. Township and county music festivals, largely organized and carried on by local supervisors of music, are much more common now than was the case but a few years ago. The radio has contributed enormously to cultural advancement in rural districts.

However valuable the facilities mentioned may be they remain more or less indirect in their cultural and educational influence. There is still a great need for more adequate education in music, particularly in the rural schools. With it should come greater opportunities for students to enjoy direct participation. The organization of glee clubs, school choirs, orchestras, and bands in rural districts provides a very desirable and much needed social activity that can enlist the enthusiasm and support of the entire community.

Many rural school teachers hesitate to introduce music into their schools because they feel the lack of sufficient training. A careful study of the rudiments of music and the chapters devoted to outlines and procedures in this book should however supply all necessary information and encourage such teachers to make the effort. The way will not be difficult and the rewards in pleasure and accomplishment great.

The procedures given in previous chapters will require modification when applied to one- or two-room rural schools, because of the varied ages of the children. For instance, songs suitable to very young children can hardly be expected to interest students in the upper grades. Where there are several grades in one room the selection of songs and the presenta-tion of facts regarding the notation of music, rhythm, and design, should be governed in general by whether the majority are older or younger pupils. If the majority are upper-grade students, more direct methods may be used in teaching the phases of music just mentioned. For the younger children give sufficient additional explanation and use such expedients as will impress these facts upon their minds.

In a rural school having a fairly large number of students, the selection of song material must be such as to meet the needs of three distinct groups —the primary, intermediate, and upper grades. Numerous patriotic, religious, and folk songs may be found that will have a common appeal to all of these groups. It will be necessary nevertheless to supply particular songs especially adapted for use by each of the separate groups and as far as possible secure the cooperation of all in learning and singing them. Students of the intermediate grades, for instance, may join in the singing of certain primary songs if they are presented to them as studies in sight singing or rhythm. In a given song the activities of each group may also be diversified according to age and ability, some marching, some counting or interpreting, while others sing. Another plan for holding the attention and developing alertness is to divide the class into groups, and have the groups sing alternate phrases of a song, the younger children the first phrase, the older pupils the second, and so on; or the smallest children may sing while the pupils of the middle grades lightly tap the rhythm and the older pupils mark the accents on the blackboard; or the older boys may whistle the melody while the others sing the words.

The comparative isolation of a rural community tends to promote a greater spirit of mutual helpfulness among the children than is true in urban communities. Thus the problems presented through having students of various ages and grades in a single class are much less difficult to solve than would appear. The real handicaps faced by the teacher are more likely to be those concerned with inadequate equipment, limited time allotment for music, and shorter terms. It is also true that in type, difficulty, and character the songs selected for use in small rural schools cannot be chosen according to the age and ability of the pupils of a single grade as in large urban graded schools but must be selected according to the varied ages and interests of the class considered as a whole. This necessarily limits very strictly the number of songs that can be taught which are specifically adapted to the separate grades.

Since the students in rural districts return to the same room in successive years the great need for a constant supply of fresh musical material is obvious. The children cannot be asked to sing or even to listen year after year to the same songs. A song book of the most comprehensive type is required if the class is to receive the variety of musical experience necessary to maintain their interest and assure progress.

The teacher should not expect miracles either from herself or the students but should be content if there is some progress to be noted from week to week and month to month. The principal objective is enjoyment of music and if in addition the pupils show a growing skill and appreciation and increased practical knowledge of the art, the teacher may be certain the music period is worth while.

PART TWO

Daily Lesson Plans
for Rural Schools

IMPORTANT

SUBSTITUTIONS for the songs named may be made from any song book available—in fact, after the first year, for the sake of variety, new songs *should* be used. The selections specified are of the *type* required and are included in the section following these outlines where the teacher may see the *kind* of material deemed best for a given purpose. Most of the songs recommended were selected from *The Silver Book of Songs* so that schools which find it necessary to supply themselves with books may obtain all the essential material in a single source.

September

First Week

MONDAY:

1. Lead the pupils in singing a familiar song. Be sure the tones are light, never harsh.

2. Teach *The Windmill*[1] as a rote song. (See Chapter IV.)

3. Use one of the musical calls given on page 10.

4. Close with another familiar song or repeat the one used at the beginning.

TUESDAY:

1. Review the song taught yesterday.

2. For unification of voices sing a three-tone series such as 1, 2, 3—3, 2, 1, using the syllable *loo*. Then have the class sing it.

3. Teach the following by rote:

Books a - way
1   2   3

Time to play
3   2   1

Mark the direction of the melody by movement of the hand.

4. To secure individual work, ask someone to sing the above phrases alone. Encourage the children to create their own words to sing with similar tone groups.

5. Teach the song, *He Didn't Think*[2].

WEDNESDAY:

1. Review musical calls.

2. Read the words of *America, the Beauful*[3].

3. Teach the first stanza by rote. Use phonograph if necessary.

4. Have the class sing *He Didn't Think*.

THURSDAY:

1. Have the class sing the first stanza of *America, the Beautiful.*

2. Review ear training exercises on the tones 1, 2, 3, which were given on Tuesday.

3. Sing the following and have the class imitate:

See the frogs wink their eyes

All the frog-gies look so wise.

4. As a rhythmic drill (see Chapter VII), have the younger children sing the song *The Windmill*, while the older children mark the rhythm by swinging their arms to the music as suggested on page 44.

FRIDAY:

1. For a listening lesson, use *In a Clock Store*[4]. Tell the story of this number before playing the record. Have the children tell how many times the clocks strike, what the boy forgot to do, and what time of day it was. Any other descriptive selection may be used on which suitable questions may be based.

A review of the week's work may be substituted for the listening lesson.

[1]p. 110, [2]p. 106, [3]p. 146, [4]Victor Record 35792.

Second Week

MONDAY:

1. Have the class sing a familiar song.

2. For tone matching and ear training give new "calls."

3. For further ear training sing the following and have the children imitate. Be sure to sing the tone groups rhythmically.

loo, loo, loo, loo, loo
1   2   3   4   5

loo, loo, loo, loo, loo
5   4   3   2   1

4. Ask if anyone knows a song in which a similar grouping of tones occurs. The answer should be, "The Windmill."

5. Review last Thursday's work in rhythm.

6. Teach by rote Bow, Wow, Wow![5]

TUESDAY:

1. Sing a familiar song.

2. Teach by rote Good Morning, Merry Sunshine[6].

3. Review No. 3 of yesterday's work. Go over it two or three times.

4. Sing and have the class repeat:

Now our work is done,
1   2   3   4   5

We will have some fun.
5   4   3   2   1

5. Have pupils step the beats in each measure of America, the Beautiful. Be sure that there is a step for each beat.

WEDNESDAY:

1. Review the song taught yesterday.

2. Teach the words and music of Row, Row, Row Your Boat[7]. This is to be sung as a unison song for the present and used as a round later in the year.

3. Review The Windmill. Compare the first phrase of it with the sentence song used yesterday.

THURSDAY:

1. Teach by rote Twenty Froggies Went to School[8].

2. Review ear training. Have two or three children sing the exercises alone.

3. Review first stanza of America, the Beautiful or sing some other song previously learned.

FRIDAY:

1. After a short review of the week's work, allow the pupils to choose and sing a few of the songs they have learned.

Third Week

MONDAY:

1. Have the class sing a song previously learned. Keep the tone quality light and beautiful.

2. For ear training, sing and then have the children repeat the following:

loo, loo, loo, loo, loo, loo, loo, loo
1 2 3 4 5 6 7 8

loo, loo, loo, loo, loo, loo, loo, loo
8 7 6 5 4 3 2 1

3. Have the class sing Row, Row, Row Your Boat. Then have the girls sing it alone. Next, have the boys sing it alone, and finally have all repeat it together.

4. Have individual children sing various tone groups previously learned, have them sing a verse of a song, or they may step the quarter-notes of a song.

TUESDAY:

1. Have the class sing Twenty Froggies Went to School.

2. Teach a seasonal song. A favorite which may be used later for dramatization is Autumn Leaves Are Falling[9].

[5]p. 103, [6]p. 150, [7]p. 121, [8]p. 113, [9]p. 108.

3. Review yesterday's ear training. Again have the children step the notes of *America, the Beautiful.* Then have them sing the song. An older pupil may be chosen to direct the singing.

WEDNESDAY:

1. Review some of the previous ear training drills.

2. Continue practice of the song, *Autumn Leaves Are Falling.*

3. Have the class sing *America, the Beautiful.* As they sing have them listen closely to the various tone lengths. There are four kinds of notes in the song; those that have one-half of a beat, one beat, one beat and a half, and three beats. Help the children to discover instances of the employment of each one of the various tone lengths. They can do this by clapping or tapping the beats of various measures.

4. Divide the class into two groups, children of grades I-III in one group, and those of grades IV-VIII in the other. Let each sing a favorite song while the other group listens.

THURSDAY:

1. Sing a song chosen by the children.

2. Review ear training and rhythm work.

3. Teach *Marching Song*[10].

4. Sing *Autumn Leaves Are Falling* and dramatize it. (See page 42.) Have the class suggest other ways of dramatizing the song.

FRIDAY:

1. For a listening lesson, play *Cradle Song (Brahms)*[11]. Call attention to the characteristic rhythm and compare it to the rhythms of other songs familiar to the children.

2. Play *March of the Tin Soldiers*[12]. Have the children lightly tap the rhythm on their desks.

Fourth Week

MONDAY:

1. Sing any song previously learned.

2. Give ear training using new tone groups from unfamiliar songs.

3. Teach by rote *The Bells*[13].

4. Have the class sing *Marching Song.*

TUESDAY:

1. Sing *Autumn Leaves Are Falling.*

2. Review *The Bells* and *He Didn't Think.*

3. Have individual pupils sing various calls and other tone groups as a review in ear training.

WEDNESDAY:

1. Teach by rote *In September*[14], and have the pupils note the different tone lengths.

2. Have older children mark the direction of the melody on the blackboard as illustrated on page 24.

3. Dramatize the song *Bow, Bow, Bow!* (See page 44.)

4. Close the lesson with a song chosen by the children.

THURSDAY:

1. Have the class sing a song chosen by the younger children.

2. To instill confidence have individual pupils sing the song alone.

3. Teach the sol-fa syllables by rote as a second stanza to *In September.*

FRIDAY:

1. For a listening lesson, play the *Tenth Regiment March*[15]. Beat the time while the pupils lightly tap the rhythm on their desks.

---

[10]p. 170, [11]Victor Record 20174, [12]V.R. 20399, [13]p. 116, [14]p. 101, [15]V.R. 20400.

2. Play the old Welsh folk song *All Through the Night*[16]. Explain that true folk songs are songs of unknown origin which have been handed down from one generation to another.. All races possess

their characteristic folk music which expresses differences in temperament, environment, and culture. Repeat the song and have the children hum the melody as it is played.

[16]Victor Record 22082.

October*

First Week

MONDAY:

1. Have the class sing a familiar song. Be sure that perfect rhythm is maintained.
2. Teach *The Goblin Man*[1].
3. Have the class sing *Row, Row, Row Your Boat*.

TUESDAY:

1. Review yesterday's lesson.
2. Review work in ear training.
3. Review rhythm work.
4. Teach *The Bridge of Avignon*[2].

WEDNESDAY:

1. Have the class sing *Twenty Froggies Went to School*.
2. Give some new tone groups for ear training.
3. Have the class sing *America, the Beautiful* and show the pupils how to beat the time. Remember that this song begins on an "up" beat—the fourth. (See page 28.)

THURSDAY:

1. Have the class sing a familiar song.
2. Review ear training given yesterday.
3. Teach *My Little Pony*[3].

FRIDAY:

1. Permit the pupils to sing several of their favorite songs.
2. Review *The Bridge of Avignon* and *My Little Pony*.

Second Week

MONDAY:

1. For rhythmic drill have the class beat the time of a familiar song.
2. Dramatize *The Windmill*. (See page 44.) Also repeat the dramatization of *Bow, Wow, Wow!*
3. Have the pupils picture on the blackboard the direction of the melodies as illustrated on page 24.
4. Sing any song previously learned. Allow the pupils to choose it.

TUESDAY:

1. Sing a familiar song.
2. Introduce the use of the observation song. Write *In September; Good Morning, Merry Sunshine*, or any other easy observation song on the blackboard in staff notation but without the time signature. Follow the procedure given on pages 23-26. Leave the song on the blackboard for later use.

WEDNESDAY:

1. Sing a song previously learned.
2. Review the song written on the blackboard yesterday, singing it with the syllable *loo*. Continue the observation song procedure.
3. Sing several of the tone groups and phrases in the song, and have individual pupils locate them on the blackboard.

*Much of the material suggested during this month is suitable for a Halloween program.
[1]p. 164, [2]p. 107, [3]p. 110.

THURSDAY:

1. Have the class sing the observation song begun on Tuesday in as finished and beautiful a manner as possible.

2. Write on the blackboard phrases, tone groups, or intervals from songs which have not yet been studied and have the class sing them.

3. Teach by rote *Jack-O'-Lantern Gay*[4].

4. Dramatize *The Goblin Man*. Have the children suggest their own interpretation or use directions on page 46.

FRIDAY:

1. For a listening lesson, use *Songs of Our Native Birds, Nos. 1 and 2*[5] by Charles Kellogg. Interesting facts about Charles Kellogg told by the teacher and the showing of pictures of the birds whose calls are reproduced will help to make an attractive program.

Third Week

MONDAY:

1. Have an older pupil place in staff notation on the blackboard the tone group

"How do you do"

1   3   5   8

and drill on the tone relationship.

2. Place a new observation song on the blackboard and use the same procedure as used for the first observation song.

3. Close the lesson with the singing of a favorite song.

TUESDAY:

1. Teach the first stanza of *America*[6]. Insist upon clear enunciation. The study of this song may be correlated with the work of the older students in history and geography.

2. Continue procedure with the observation song on the blackboard.

3. Have individual students sing songs previously learned.

WEDNESDAY:

1. Have the class sing the first stanza of *America*.

2. Develop the tone groups 1 - 3 - 5 - 8 into a question and answer song. (See page 67.)

3. Review ear training and rhythm work on the phrases and tone groups given last Thursday.

4. Teach by rote *Jolly Is the Miller*[7].

5. Sing *The Bells*.

THURSDAY:

1. Have the class sing *Jack-O'-Lantern Gay* and *The Goblin Man*.

2. Begin development of free rhythmic expression. (See page 31.)

3. Continue work on the observation song.

FRIDAY:

1. As preparation for a Halloween event have the children sing any songs they may know which are suited for use in a program.

2. Continue work on the observation song.

3. Review *Jolly Is the Miller* and other songs learned during the month.

Fourth Week

MONDAY:

1. Select and have the class sing a bright lively song. Watch the pitch and tone quality.

2. Give a short drill on the recognition of tone groups selected from songs not yet learned.

3. Close by having the class sing *The Windmill*, paying particular attention to its pronounced rhythm.

TUESDAY:

1. Have the pupils choose and sing several songs.

---

[4]p. 109, [5]Victor Record 35785, [6]p. 145, [7]p. 104.

2. Give drill in free rhythmic expression.

3. Introduce *The Windmill* as an observation song.

WEDNESDAY:

1. Review tone groups used in the drill on Monday.

2. Teach the first stanza of *The Star-Spangled Banner*[8]. In beating the time remember that this song begins on the third beat—an "up" beat. Describe the circumstances connected with the origin of this song.

3. Continue work with *The Windmill* as an observation song.

[8]p. 144.

THURSDAY:

1. Have the class sing *America*.

2. Give a short drill on tone groups from unfamiliar songs.

3. Continue procedure on *The Windmill*. Also have the pupils clap the beats of each measure and then clap the notes as the teacher counts the beats.

FRIDAY:

1. As a lesson in music appreciation correlate music with geography, selecting a suitable phonograph record for the purpose. (See page 100.)

November*

First Week

MONDAY:

1. Teach *First Snow*[1].

2. Teach the singing game, *The Mulberry Bush*[2]. (See page 35.)

3. Give a short review of an observation song.

TUESDAY:

1. Have the class sing a familiar song.

2. Introduce the staff by placing it on the blackboard with the sol-fa syllables on it. Stress the number of lines and spaces.

3. Teach *The Pumpkin and the Turkey*.[3]

4. With books before them have the children sing *The Windmill* or any other simple song previously learned by rote. Have them point to each phrase as they sing.

WEDNESDAY:

1. As creative work have the older pupils write on the blackboard, in staff notation, simple melodies for question and answer phrases. (See page 67.)

2. Sing *The Pumpkin and the Turkey* and other songs previously learned.

THURSDAY:

1. Place a new observation song on the blackboard and follow the usual procedure. Be sure to select one which contains familiar tone groups and phrases.

2. Have the class sing the song with the sol-fa syllables.

3. Sing a familiar song.

FRIDAY:

1. Give a short drill on an observation song.

2. For a lesson in appreciation use *Old Folks at Home*[4].

3. Have the students sing the song with the phonograph.

Second Week

MONDAY:

1. Teach the first stanza of the Thanksgiving song, *Over the River and Through the Wood*[5].

*At the end of this month it may be desirable to give a Thanksgiving program. Many of the songs suggested for study during the month are appropriate for this purpose.
[1]p. 120, [2]p. 105, [3]p. 151, [4]Victor Record 21950, [5]p. 131.

2. Have the children write on the blackboard in staff notation familiar tone groups from various songs. Then have the children sing them.

3. Have the pupils step the notes of *In September* or any other song containing a majority of quarter-notes, giving a step to each beat. Count two measures aloud to establish the tempo. The first beat of each measure should be accented by a heavy step. The pupils stand still and count during the rests. On the dotted half-note the step should be 1 - front, 2 - side, 3 - together.

4. Finish development of the observation song introduced on Thursday.

TUESDAY:

1. Review beating time by having half of the class beat the time while the other half sings. Use songs previously learned. Watch for inaccuracies in rhythm and pitch and stress tone quality.

2. Teach a new round as a unison song. It will be sung as a round later.

3. Review the first stanza of *Over the River and Through the Wood*. Then have the children step or tap the notes.

WEDNESDAY:

1. Sing *America*. If the fourth stanza is sung the first half should be sung softly and reverently and then with increased volume in the last half.

2. Teach the younger children *The Pop Corn Song*[6].

3. Introduce and develop a new observation song.

4. Close with a song selected by the class.

THURSDAY:

1. Have the class practice the scale by singing in two-four time as follows: *do - do, re - re, mi - mi,* and so on.

2. Teach the second stanza of *Over the River and Through the Wood*.

3. Sing any song previously learned.

FRIDAY:

1. Give a lesson in rhythm using a record in which strongly marked rhythms are featured. *Rhythms for Children*[7] is very good. Have it serve as the accompaniment for a rhythmic "Follow the Leader" game. Choose a leader who possesses good rhythmic perception. Whatever he does in response to the music—clapping, stepping, swinging arms in circles in the air, beating time, or marking lines on the blackboard—should be imitated by the other pupils.

The principal accents should receive a loud clap and the secondary accents a soft clap.

In marking the accents by means of lines on the blackboard the accented notes are indicated by long lines and the other notes by short ones, in this manner:

Third Week

MONDAY:

1. Review *First Snow*.

2. Rehearse the first two stanzas of *Over the River and Through the Wood,* and teach the third stanza.

3. Complete the work on the observation song started last Wednesday.

TUESDAY:

1. Have the younger children dramatize *The Pop Corn Song* while the older children sing it.

2. Introduce the study song, using *A Thankful Song*[8]. (See page 27.) This

[6]p. 158, [7]Victor Record 22168, [8]p. 116.

first study song may be placed on the blackboard for development before singing it from the books, but subsequent ones should be taught from the books in the hands of the pupils. Remind the children that as *do* changes its location on the staff the position of the other syllables is also changed.

WEDNESDAY:

1. As a step in creative music help the children to compose musical calls on the skips 1 - 3 - 5 - 8 (*do - mi - sol - do*), on short tone groups in scale order, and on various other tone groups. (See page 67.)

2. Sing *Over the River and Through the Wood* and *A Thankful Song*.

THURSDAY:

1. Let the pupils choose an opening song.

2. Sing *The Star-Spangled Banner* giving particular attention to clear enunciation.

3. Give ear training or rhythm drill.

4. Close with the singing of *America*.

FRIDAY:

1. For an opening song use one learned early in the year.

2. Give a short drill on some technical work such as writing intervals and tone groups and reading them with syllables.

3. If pupils' progress is such that it seems desirable, the names of the lines and spaces of the treble staff may be presented at this time. If not, this may be deferred. (See fourth week of February outline.)

4. For closing, sing another song learned early in the year.

Fourth Week

MONDAY:

1. Teach by rote *The Grocer and the Housewife*[9].

2. Review *A Thankful Song*. If the dot has not been previously explained, call attention to the dotted note in the last measure and explain that a dot after a note increases its duration one-half.

3. Sing any song being learned for a Thanksgiving program.

TUESDAY:

1. Sing *The Grocer and the Housewife*.

2. Have the scale of C written on the blackboard. All sing it, using syllables.

3. Introduce the key of F and explain that *do* of the new key is the fourth tone of the scale of C. (See page 191.) Play the new scale without flatting the fourth tone and ask the children to tell which tone needs to be changed. Then play it correctly and have the class sing it with the syllables.

4. Teach *The Cuckoo*[10], using syllables, and develop it as a study song.

WEDNESDAY:

1. If a Thanksgiving program has been planned, give it today. If it is to be given after school hours use the music period for rehearsal.

THURSDAY: (Thanksgiving Day)

FRIDAY:

1. Continue development of *The Cuckoo*.

2. Teach *Ten Little Indians*[11].

3. Play records or sing songs.

[9]p. 116, [10]p. 113, [11]p. 112.

December*

First Week

MONDAY:

1. Give rhythm drills and sing tone groups to unify voices.
2. Teach *Silent Night*[1].
3. Have the pupils mark the direction of the melody on the blackboard.

TUESDAY:

1. Continue practice of *Silent Night*.
2. Review rhythm and ear training work.
3. Have older pupils sing the first measure of *Silent Night* and younger pupils the second measure as an echo. Older group then sings third measure and younger group the fourth measure. Older group sings measures five and six; younger group, seven and eight. Last four measures are sung in unison.

WEDNESDAY:

1. Teach the round, *Christmas Bells (Are You Sleeping, Brother John?)*[2]. First sing it as a unison song and then as a round with the class divided into three sections. Have a competent leader for each section and watch that perfect rhythm is maintained.
2. Teach the second stanza of *Silent Night*.

THURSDAY:

1. Give a short drill on skips such as 1 - 3 - 5 - 8 (*do - mi - sol - do*). Next sing the group 8 - 7 - 8 with *loo*, and have the pupils sing the same group with syllables (*do - ti - do*). Lead the children to find these and other familiar tone groups in songs they are learning.
2. Call upon individual students to sing phrases of Christmas songs.
3. Teach the third stanza of *Silent Night*.

FRIDAY:

1. Give a talk on Christmas carols with stories of their origins. Much interesting material may be found in "The Christmas Carolers' Book in Song and Story"[3].
2. Have the class sing *Silent Night*, paying special attention to tone quality and expression.

Second Week

MONDAY:

1. Teach the first stanza of *It Came Upon the Midnight Clear*[4] or any other popular Christmas song.
2. Review rhythm work and ear training.
3. Have the class sing *Christmas Bells*, as a round if possible, otherwise in unison.

TUESDAY:

1. Teach *Jolly Old St. Nicholas*[5].
2. Review the key of F. Teach the older students to locate *do* on the staff. Remind the class that the key of F, with one flat, begins on the fourth tone of the C scale.
3. Demonstrate that these scales, C and F, are made up of the following intervals: 1 - 2 (whole-step), 2 - 3 (whole-step), 3 - 4 (half-step), 4 - 5 (whole-step), 5 - 6 (whole-step), 6 - 7 (whole-step), 7 - 8 (half-step). Explain that all scales so constructed are called major scales.
4. Rehearse the Christmas songs.

WEDNESDAY:

1. Review the notation of the scale of F.
2. Have older pupils write on the blackboard various tone groups from familiar songs in the key of F.
3. Practice the Christmas songs.

---

*All of the songs included in the plans for December are Christmas songs, so that by Christmas time the children will have a repertoire suitable for a Christmas program.
[1]p. 137, [2]p. 125, [3]Published by Hall & McCreary Company, [4]p. 139, [5]p. 115.

THURSDAY:

1. Teach *O Come, All Ye Faithful*[6].
2. Review the scale of F.
3. Practice the Christmas songs.

FRIDAY:

1. Have the children sing Christmas songs of their own choosing previously learned in the class.
2. For a listening lesson play *Chrismas Hymns and Carols*[7].

Third Week

MONDAY:

1. Review the Christmas songs.
2. Divide the class into two groups and have them sing *Silent Night* antiphonally—that is, one group sings the first phrase, the other group the second phrase, and so on throughout the song.
3. Teach the song *Santa's Cake*[8].

TUESDAY:

1. Select a song and have the class tap the beats and then the notes.
2. Practice the Christmas songs.
3. Have the younger children dramatize *Jolly Old St. Nicholas*. (See page 45.)

[6]p. 140, [7]Victor Records 35788 and 35946, [8]p. 161, [9]p. 141.

WEDNESDAY:

1. Teach the carol, *The First Noel*[9].
2. All tap or mark the time.
3. Continue work on the other Christmas songs.

THURSDAY:

1. As a step in part singing divide the class into two sections and have the first section sing the scale of C (*do - re - mi - fa - sol - la - ti - do*). Then have the second section sing a similar series beginning on *mi* (*mi - fa - sol - la - ti - do - re - mi*).
2. Have the two groups sing their respective scales together. (See page 29.) Repeat this twice and be sure that each section is accurate as to time and pitch.
3. Work on the Christmas songs.

FRIDAY:

1. Review the Christmas songs and rehearse the Christmas program if one is planned.

(In the event there are several more days of school prior to Christmas and the holiday vacation period extends into January, the work outlined for the first days of January may be used for the remaining days of December.)

January

First Week

MONDAY:

1. Have the class sing *America*.
2. Have the class sing a scale in thirds as on Thursday. (See page 29.)
3. For ear training have pupils sing the tones of the major chord 1 - 3 - 5 - 8 (*do - mi - sol - do*) and 8 - 5 - 3 - 1 (*do - sol - mi - do*); then use other tone groups for this drill.
4. Teach as a new study song, *Cold's the Wind*[1].

[1]p. 129, [2]p. 102.

TUESDAY:

1. Have the class sing a song previously learned.
2. Continue the study of *Cold's the Wind*.
3. Select and sing a song which correlates with some subject being taught.
4. Teach by rote *Wind the Bobbin*[2].

WEDNESDAY:

1. Allow the class to choose an opening song.

2. Use *The Swallows*[3] as a reading song. (See page 27.)

3. Introduce the scale of G and explain that *do* of the new key is the fifth tone of the scale of C. Have the children locate G on the staff. Play the scale slowly from G without the sharp and ask the pupils to locate the tone that needs to be changed. Then play it with the seventh (F) sharped in correct order.

4. Have the students recite the letter names of the scales of F and G and review the intervals between the successive tones of the major scale. Explain the necessity for sharps and flats in order to provide the half-steps between 3 and 4, and 7 and 8 of the scale.

5. Close with the first stanza of *The Star-Spangled Banner*.

THURSDAY:

1. Let the class choose the opening song.

2. Give a short drill on tone groups in the new key, G: the scale ascending and descending; skips, 1 - 3 - 5 - 8 - 5 - 3 - 1 (*do - mi - sol - do - sol - mi - do*) and 1 - 3 - 4 - 2 - 1 (*do - mi - fa - re - do*).

3. Have older pupils write on the blackboard in staff notation the skips 1 - 3 - 5 - 8 and other familiar tone groups in the key of G.

4. Review *The Swallows*.

FRIDAY:

1. Teach by rote the first stanza of *There Are Many Flags in Many Lands*[4].

2. Have the class tap the beats and then the notes of *Cold's the Wind*.

3. Dramatize *Wind the Bobbin*.

Second Week

MONDAY:

1. Begin the lesson by having the class sing a favorite song.

2. Teach by rote the first stanza and chorus of *Old Black Joe*[5]. Have the pupils tap the beats and carefully observe the holds and expression marks.

3. Close with the class singing the first two stanzas of *America, the Beautiful*.

TUESDAY:

1. Review the first stanza of *There Are Many Flags in Many Lands*.

2. Select a song which has been taught by rote but one of which the pupils have not seen the notation. Before the lesson period write the notation on the blackboard. Tell the children it is a song they have been singing, and have them examine the notation phrase by phrase. Use a pointer to indicate the phrases. Lead then to a recognition of the song, and then have them sing it, pointing to each note as it is sung. Have an older pupil point to the notes while the song is repeated by the class.

3. Ask individuals to point out on the blackboard all the *sols, dos, mis*, various note values, ties, and so on.

WEDNESDAY:

1. Allow the class to choose an opening song.

2. Discuss the number of beats to a measure including two-, three-, four-, and six-beat measures in familiar rote songs.

3. Review *Cold's the Wind* and *A Thankful Song*.

THURSDAY:

1. Give individual drill in singing tone groups, and then have pupils write them on the staff.

2. Teach *Bobby Shafto*[6] as a study song.

3. Sing first stanza and chorus of *Old Black Joe*.

---

[3]p. 119, [4]p. 135, [5]p. 136, [6]p. 108.

FRIDAY:

1. Review the scales of C, G, and F by having certain pupils give the pitch names and others write the scales on the blackboard. Then have them write various tone groups in these keys.

2. Sing a round. The younger children may tap the beats lightly on their desks while the others sing.

3. Permit the children to choose a song for dramatization.

Third Week

MONDAY:

1. Teach the class a singing game such as *A-Hunting We Will Go*[7]. (See page 35.)

2. Introduce the scale of D and help the children to find the keynote.

3. Play the scale from D without using the sharps and have the class decide what changes in the tones are necessary to make a satisfactory major scale.

4. Write the scale of D on the blackboard but without the key signature or sharps being placed before the proper notes. Then ask which notes of the scale are sharped. When F and C are named by letter, place the sharps before the notes on the staff. Then explain why and how the sharps are grouped at the beginning as a key signature. As this is being explained, erase the sharps before the notes and place them in proper position at the beginning of the staff, noting that the F♯ is placed on the fifth line and the C♯ in the third space. Further explain that all tones having letter names corresponding to the tones which are altered by the signature are affected regardless of the position of the notes, whether on, above, or below the staff.

5. Have the children discover songs in the key of D in their song books and sing a familiar one in this key.

TUESDAY:

1. Select and teach a new singing game.
2. Sing a round.
3. Use *First Snow* as a reading song.

WEDNESDAY:

1. Read *The Snowflakes' Race*[8] using syllables and develop as a study song. Observe eighth-notes, quarter-notes, eighth-rest, quarter-rests, similar tone groups, and the number of phrases.

2. Place the following group of notes on the blackboard:

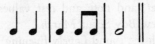

Have the pupils step these note values. (See page 40.)

3. Sing verses one and two of *There Are Many Flags in Many Lands*.

THURSDAY:

1. Use question-answer songs of the type suggested on page 11.

2. Point out the balance and contrast of phrases in familiar songs.

3. Have the class make up a couplet. (See page 68.)

4. Sing the following:
The mer - ry win - ter now is here.
8   7   6 5   4   3 2 1

5. Sing *First Snow*.

FRIDAY:

1. Sing *The Snowflakes' Race*.
2. Teach by rote *Boy Scout March*[9].
3. Allow the children to sing their favorite songs, play singing games, or give song dramatizations.

---

[7]p. 107, [8]p. 106, [9]p. 174.

Fourth Week

MONDAY:

1. Have the class sing a bright lively song. Watch tone quality and enunciation. Have one of the students lead the class in the singing. The one chosen should possess a good rhythmic sense and be able to beat the time accurately.

2. Have the class sing from their books, with syllables, familiar songs in the keys of C, G, F, and D.

3. Have the pupils make up several calls and tone groups in the four keys.

TUESDAY:

1. Teach the song *A Sailor Dear*[10] by rote to the younger children, while the older pupils write a short test on the staff, clef, and note and rest values.

2. Review *Boy Scout March*.

3. Teach the round *Lovely Evening*[11].

WEDNESDAY:

1. Review *A Sailor Dear* and *Boy Scout March*.

2. Teach *The Man in the Moon*[12] by rote.

---

[10]p. 162, [11]p. 143, [12]p. 101, [13]Victor Record 24776.

3. Teach the key and scale of E♭ by the procedure outlined Monday of last week.

THURSDAY:

1. Use *The Bridge of Avignon* as a reading song, following procedure on page 27.

2. Divide the class into two groups of younger and older students and let each sing its favorite song.

FRIDAY:

1. Dramatize *Ten Little Indians*. (See page 46.)

2. Draw out the creative imagination of the pupils by playing on the phonograph some characteristic piece of music such as the *March of the Priests*[13] from "The Magic Flute" by Mozart. Tell the pupils to listen carefully to the music and then to describe the nature of the picture or feelings that were aroused in them. It may be advisable to play the record a second time before asking their impressions, for the strangeness of the music may mitigate against a definite reaction from a single hearing.

February

First Week

MONDAY:

1. Before the lesson begins, write *Ten Little Indians* on the blackboard in the key of A. Also write it in F as given on page 112. Have the class sing it in A as an opening song. Explain the meaning of transposition. (See page 211.) Use observation song procedure. Then have the class sing the song in F.

2. Teach the words of *Betsy Ross*[1], and give a short talk on the history of our flag.

---

[1]p. 165.

3. Review *There Are Many Flags in Many Lands*.

TUESDAY:

1. Write the scale of A on the blackboard and follow the usual procedure for introducing a new scale and key. Drill on various skips and tone groups in this key.

2. Teach by rote the music of *Betsy Ross*.

3. Close by singing *The Man in the Moon*.

WEDNESDAY:

1. Sing a patriotic song.

2. Review *Betsy Ross*.

3. Write *The Clouds*[2] on the blackboard and use it as a reading song. Follow the procedure carefully and be sure that the breath mark between "fairies" and "lay" in the last phrase is observed.

THURSDAY:

1. Have individual students sing the reading song used yesterday.

2. Have the class sing several songs previously learned, particularly those suitable for a Lincoln or Washington birthday program.

FRIDAY:

1. For correlation with history and as preparation for a Washington program, play *Hail Columbia*[3]. The music, written in 1789, is said to have been played at Washington's inauguration. The words were written in 1798 by Joseph Hopkinson, whose father was one of the first American composers.

2. Give a short talk on the symphony orchestra. (See page 64.) Play *Instruments of the Orchestra—Strings*[4], naming the instruments as they are illustrated and calling attention to the contrasting qualities of tone.

Second Week

MONDAY:

1. Review songs taught during the previous week.

2. Give a short drill on the scale of A and tone groups in this key, using the sol-fa syllables.

TUESDAY:

1. Use *A-Hunting We Will Go* as a reading song. Follow carefully the reading song procedure.

2. Point out that the four flats in the key signature indicate the song is in the key of A♭. Compare this key with the key of A. *Do* is on the second space in both keys, therefore the location of the syllables is the same for each key.

3. Teach a new stanza of *There Are Many Flags in Many Lands*.

WEDNESDAY:

1. Teach the following verse:

I love the name of Washington,
I love my country true,
I love the flag, the dear old flag—
The red, the white, and blue.

2. Teach the tune *Auld Lang Syne*[5] without the chorus and have it sung with the verse just given.

3. Have individual students sing songs previously learned.

4. Review *A-Hunting We Will Go*.

THURSDAY:

1. Teach by rote *Little George Washington*[6].

2. As ear training have individual pupils identify short tone groups by giving either syllable or number names.

3. Have older pupils write scales and tone groups in various keys on the blackboard.

FRIDAY:

1. Continue the talk on the orchestra begun last Friday, and illustrate by using Victor Records 20522 and 20523.

Play *Narcissus* and have individual students tell their impressions of the music.

For contrast play *The Hunt in the Black Forest*. (See page 59.)

[2]p. 114, [3]Victor Record 22013, [4]V.R. 20522, [5]No. 131, The Silver Book of Songs—V.R. 22082, [6]p. 153.

Third Week

MONDAY:

1. Review songs learned last week.
2. Teach *The Happy Farmer*[7] by rote.
3. Teach the music of the round, *Three Blind Mice*[8]. Have the class learn the verse "George Washington" which follows and sing it to this tune.

> George Washington
> Couldn't tell a lie.
> He cut down a tree
> With his father's axe
> And went to war
> On account of the tax,
> And these are all the important facts
> Of George Washington.
>
> —Anonymous

TUESDAY:

1. Review *The Happy Farmer* and other songs studied last week.
2. As ear training have individual pupils identify tone groups by syllable or number.
3. Have the class compose music for a couplet. (See page 68.)
4. Have the children dramatize a song or learn a folk dance.

WEDNESDAY:

1. Review the songs learned on Monday.
2. Using syllables, read songs in several of the keys that have been learned.
3. Have older pupils put on a staff on the blackboard the signatures of various keys and identify them.

THURSDAY:

1. Teach the old Swedish singing game *I See You*[9]. (See page 33.)
2. Review *Lovely Evening*

FRIDAY:

1. Teach the folk song *In Finland*[10].
2. Continue last Friday's study of the instruments of the orchestra.

Fourth Week

MONDAY:

1. Review *Bobby Shafto* and *The Clouds*.
2. Use as a reading song *The Boys of the Zuider Zee*[11].

TUESDAY:

1. Have the class review the reading song begun yesterday.
2. For ear training use tone groups of four or five tones and have individual students identify them by syllables and numbers, or by writing them on the staff.
3. Teach the class the letter names of the lines and spaces of the staff. First teach the lines, then the spaces, beginning with the lowest line or space. Then teach the letter names of the first space below and the first space above the staff and that Middle C is on the first leger line below. Place each letter on the correct line or space as it is named. Also teach the number names of the lines of the staff from the lowest to the highest (from one to five) and the spaces within the staff (from one to four). (See illustration on page 182.)

WEDNESDAY:

1. Have the class review *My Little Pony* and the first stanza of *The Boys of the Zuider Zee*.
2. Review letter names of the lines and spaces of the staff.
3. Teach the first stanza of *Old Folks at Home*[12].
4. Clap or tap the notes and beats of songs recently learned.

THURSDAY:

1. Review *In Finland*.
2. Have the class name the notes of a song which has been placed on the blackboard or of familiar songs in their books.

[7]p. 124, [8]p. 114, [9]p. 102, [10]p. 123, [11]p. 122, [12]p. 138.

3. Teach the second stanza of *The Boys of the Zuider Zee*.

4. Let the class choose a closing song.

FRIDAY:

1. Give a prepared or impromptu musical program or play instrumental records and identify each selection as it is played by giving its name and composer and the kind of instruments used. This is essential in preparation for music recognition tests which should come later. If available use the *Overture to William Tell*[13], pointing out especially that portion descriptive of the storm, in which the lightning is suggested by the quick short tones of the piccolo and flute, the thunder by the kettle drums, the rain by the descending scale, and the wind by the ascending scale.

[13]Victor Record 20606.

March

First Week

MONDAY:

1. Review a few songs in the key of A♭. Next write on the blackboard in this key short phrases from familiar songs that are in other keys. These may be taken from the pupils' books. Then proceed with further explanation of transposition.

2. Point out to the class that the sharps and flats in key signatures are placed according to the order of their appearance in the scale system. The sharp furthest to the right (the last one added to the signature) is always on the *seventh tone* and therefore the *do* and letter name of the key and scale is on the line or space one degree higher.

The flat furthest to the right (the last one added to the signature) is always on the *fourth tone* and therefore the *do* and letter name of the key and scale is on the line or space four degrees lower.

3. Teach the music and first stanza of the song *Pussy Willows*[1].

TUESDAY:

1. Through the reading of *Old March Wind*[2], introduce the key of E (four sharps). Follow the usual procedure.

2. Teach the sol-fa syllables of the first phrase of *Old March Wind*, and have the children find another phrase of the song that is like it except for a different rhythmic figure on the second and fourth beats of the measure.

3. Review *Pussy Willows* and also have the song sung with sol-fa syllables. Point out that the syllable names have the same location on the staff as in *Old March Wind*.

4. Let the pupils point out the different note values, phrases and rhythmic figures in the two songs.

WEDNESDAY:

1. Review *Old March Wind*, singing it with *loo*. When the children can sing the melody correctly with *loo*, they may then sing the song using the words.

2. Teach other stanzas of *Pussy Willows*.

3. Have individual children sing songs, tone groups, phrases, and scales, and give the letter names of staff lines and spaces.

THURSDAY:

1. Teach *The Dandelions*[3].

2. Review *Pussy Willows*.

3. Teach the round *The Lame Tame*

[1]p. 105, [2]p. 109, [3]p. 111.

Crane⁴ first as a unison song and then as a round.

FRIDAY:

1. Tell the story of one of the operas—"Hansel and Gretel" or "Lohengrin". For stories and pictures consult "The Victrola Book of the Opera". For records, see page 100.

Second Week

MONDAY:

1. Teach *The Elfin Balloon*⁵ as a reading song.
2. Do some ear-training work using phrases and tone groups from both familiar and unfamiliar songs.
3. Teach by rote *The Chinese Vegetable Man*⁶.
4. Close with a song selected by the class.

TUESDAY:

1. Have the class sing *Old Black Joe*.
2. Have the pupils point out and name the various kinds of notes and rests, the key and time signatures, and have them read the pitch names of the melody of this song.
3. Give rhythmic drill, clapping and tapping the beats and notes of *The Elfin Balloon*.

WEDNESDAY:

1. Sing *The Elfin Balloon* and *The Dandelions*.
2. Teach by rote the "stunt" song, *The Big Bad Mouse* .
3. Review *The Lame Tame Crane*.

THURSDAY:

1. Teach *Lullaby*⁸ by rote.
2. Continue practice reading the pitch names of the notes of familiar melodies.
3. Review *A Big Bad Mouse*.

FRIDAY:

1. As a listening lesson use new material drawn from the records suggested on page 100. Ask the children to name the instruments heard. Strengthen their imaginative and emotional response to the music in every way possible.

Third Week

MONDAY:

1. Review *The Big Bad Mouse, Lullaby*, or any feature of last week's work needing review.
2. With the class divided into two groups, practice singing scales in thirds.
3. Teach the spring song, *On Easter Eve*⁹ or *The Robin*¹⁰ by rote.

TUESDAY:

1. Teach the song, *Columbia, the Gem of the Ocean*¹¹.
2. Have the pupils read the pitch names of the melody notes of familiar songs.
3. Give rhythmic drill on the notes and beats of *All the Birds Are Here Again*¹².

WEDNESDAY:

1. Have the class sing *Columbia, the Gem of the Ocean*.
2. Have pupils read the pitch names and give the syllables of the two-part song, *All the Birds Are Here Again*.
3. Dictate tone groups and have individual pupils write them on the blackboard.

THURSDAY:

1. Have the class sing *All the Birds Are Here Again*.
2. Review the scales thus far learned by having individual students sing them with *loo* and the sol-fa syllables. Also have individuals sing tone groups and others recite the scales using letter names.

⁴p. 114, ⁵p. 118, ⁶p. 118, ⁷p. 155, ⁸p. 147, ⁹p. 172, ¹⁰p. 117, ¹¹p. 142, ¹²p. 126.

3. Sing a song selected by the younger children.

FRIDAY:

1. As a listening lesson illustrate contrast of mood by playing *Sweet and Low*[13] and *Tarantelle*[14].

Fourth Week

MONDAY:

1. Have the class sing *On Easter Eve* or *The Robin*.
2. Read the pitch names of the melody notes of *The Boys of the Zuider Zee*.
3. Sing *Columbia, the Gem of the Ocean*.
4. Continue work on the two-part song, *All the Birds Are Here Again*.

TUESDAY:

1. Review a singing game—*I See You* or *The Mulberry Bush*.
2. Teach *The Birds' Ball*[15].
3. Play the record *Rhythm Medley, Nos. 1 and 2*[16], and have the children tap the rhythms and imitate the motions suggested.

[13]Victor Record 20174, [14]V.R. 20079, [15]p. 134, [16]V.R. 20526.

WEDNESDAY:

1. Give a written test on signatures, letter names of scale notes, and tone groups including all the keys that have been studied. Children too young to take the test may be given staff ruled paper and asked to copy various tone groups and phrases of songs which the teacher has placed on the blackboard especially for them.

THURSDAY:

1. Continue work on the song *The Birds' Ball*.
2. Review some of the songs learned during February and March.
3. Review rhythm activities such as stepping notes, clapping rhythm, or using singing games.

FRIDAY:

1. As a test play a portion of each of several records used in recent Friday lesson periods, and after each is played have the pupils write the title of the composition and the name of the composer.

April

First Week

MONDAY:

1. Sing a song chosen by the older students.
2. Teach *Swinging*[1] or a song of the same type, in the key of A.
3. Have a student place the notes representing *do - mi - sol* in the key of A on the blackboard. Then as a means of introducing the key of B♭, have *do, mi,* and *sol* put on the blackboard represented by notes on the third, fourth and fifth lines respectively. Place a flat before the note

representing the new *do*, name the key as the key of B♭. Then give the pitch and have the song *Swinging* sung in the new key. Explain that the song has been transposed to a key whose *do* is one half-step higher and on the next degree above the *do* of the key of A. Write the song on the blackboard in both keys and compare the position of the notes.

4. Practice the song *The Birds' Ball*.

TUESDAY:

1. Have individual students write the scale of B♭ on the blackboard and recite

[1]p. 119.

the letter names of the tones. Point out that the second space below the staff is B, and have the scale written from there.

2. Teach by rote *The Rainbow Song*[2].

3. Have the class sing *Columbia, the Gem of the Ocean.*

WEDNESDAY:

1. Teach by rote the sailors' chantey *Blow the Man Down*[3].

2. Continue work with the record *Rhythm Medley, Nos. 1 and 2*, having the pupils mark the rhythms and imitate the motions suggested.

3. Have the pupils read the pitch names and give the syllables of the three-part song, *Summer-Night's Dream*[4].

THURSDAY:

1. Review the scale of Bb by having individual pupils recite the notes of various tone groups using both sol-fa syllables and pitch names.

2. Practice *Blow the Man Down.*

3. Practice the three-part song, *Summer-Night's Dream.*

FRIDAY:

1. Play new records selected from the list on page 100. Identify each selection by title and composer. Also identify the instruments.

Second Week

MONDAY:

1. Review *Blow the Man Down* and *Summer-Night's Dream.*

2. Teach *Home on the Range*[5] by rote.

3. Sing a round.

TUESDAY:

1. Practice *Home on the Range.*

2. Teach the words of *I Hear a Little Tapping*[6] or *To Italy*[7].

3. Sing a familiar song.

WEDNESDAY:

1. Teach the music of the song begun yesterday.

2. Have the pupils give the pitch names and syllables of the notes of the three-part song, *Down in the Valley*[8].

3. Tap or clap the notes and beats of the song.

4. Sing the song *Home on the Range* as a closing number.

THURSDAY:

1. Let the class write a melody for a couplet or quatrain.

2. Review the song begun on Tuesday.

3. Sing *Swinging.*

FRIDAY:

1. Continue work on *Down in the Valley.*

2. Review *The Rainbow Song* and *Blow the Man Down.*

3. Spend the remainder of the lesson period playing various phonograph records requested by the pupils. Ask them to express reasons for their choice of particular selections.

Third Week

MONDAY:

1. Teach by rote, as a unison song, *April's Wand*[9]. If found suitable to the age and ability of the group this song will be excellent for use as a part song.

2. Have a short song in the key of C on the blackboard and ask the pupils to write out a transposition of it in any of the keys that have been learned.

TUESDAY:

1. Practice *April's Wand.*

2. Teach *At Sea*[10] or *Persephone's Return*[11] as a unison song.

WEDNESDAY:

1. Review *April's Wand, Persephone's Return,* or *At Sea.*

---

[2]p. 152, [3]p. 132, [4]p. 128, [5]p. 133, [6]p. 167, [7]p. 122, [8]p. 130, [9]p. 126, [10]p. 121, [11]p. 128.

2. Teach *A Frog He Would A-Wooing Go*[12].

3. Have individual pupils read the pitch names of *A Frog He Would A-Wooing Go*. If the work is divided so that each student is assigned but one or two measures better results will be obtained.

THURSDAY:

1. Have the class sing *April's Wand*.

2. Continue work on *A Frog He Would A-Wooing Go*.

3. Use *Bonny Scotsmen*[13] as a reading song. Call attention to the rhythmic figure—a characteristic of Scottish folk music called the "Scottish snap".

FRIDAY:

1. Have the class write a few of the scales studied to date.

2. For a lesson in appreciation play *Instruments of the Orchestra—Brass*[14]. Identify the instruments and call attention to their tone qualities. Show pictures of the instruments.

Fourth Week

MONDAY:

1. Review *Persephone's Return* or *At Sea*.

2. Continue work on *Bonny Scotsmen*.

12p. 124, 13p. 129, 14Victor Record 20523, 15p. 132.

3. Have pupils read the pitch names of *Bonny Scotsmen*.

TUESDAY:

1. Have the class sing *A Frog He Would A-Wooing Go*.

2. Give rhythmic drill, stepping, clapping, and tapping notes and beats of various songs.

3. Teach the round *Hey! Ho! to the Greenwood Go*[15].

WEDNESDAY:

1. Sing the rounds *Lovely Evening, The Lame Tame Crane*, and *Hey! Ho! to the Greenwood Go*.

2. Give oral test relating to the staff, scales, notes, and rests.

3. Sing *Bonny Scotsmen* and *Home on the Range*.

THURSDAY:

1. Sing songs learned during the year. Allow the students to express their choice.

FRIDAY:

1. Beginning today the music periods of the remaining days of school may be devoted to a review of the year's work or to the preparation of a closing program.

Song List for Choirs or Choruses
in Rural Schools

The songs listed below have been selected to meet the needs of rural school choirs or choruses for four successive years. In the list for each year there is material for the primary, elementary, and older pupils, and each succeeding year offers selections of increasing difficulty. These songs, like all other recommended material, are intended to be suggestive of the type to be used. They are contained in the song section of this book. If the songs are not included in the class song books you have, other attractive selections of similar character may be substituted.

First Year

	Page		Page
Bobby Shafto	108	Twenty Froggies Went to School	113
The Elfin Balloon	118	Old Folks at Home	138
The Dandelions	111	Autumn Leaves Are Falling	108
A Thankful Song	116	The Robin	117
The Windmill	110	America	145

Second Year

	Page		Page
First Snow	120	The Dancing Lesson	103
The Grocer and the Housewife	116	Good Morning, Merry Sunshine	150
A Frog He Would A-Wooing Go	124	The Bridge of Avignon	107
The Rainbow Song	152	A-Hunting We Will Go	107
The Chinese Vegetable Man	118	America, the Beautiful	146

Third Year

	Page		Page
There Are Many Flags in Many Lands	135	I Hear a Little Tapping	167
The Pop Corn Song	158	Pussy Willows	105
Lazy Robin	120	Betsy Ross	165
In Finland	123	The Star-Spangled Banner	144
		To Italy	122
		All the Birds Are Here Again	126

Fourth Year

	Page		Page
Lullaby	147	Old Black Joe	136
Boy Scout March	174	April's Wand	126
Persephone's Return	128	Summer-Night's Dream	128
Stars of the Summer Night	136	Columbia, the Gem of the Ocean	142
Down in the Valley	130	On Easter Eve	172

PART THREE

SONGS

Songs in the following section which are numbered are from *The Silver Book of Songs*. The numbers correspond to those in the song book. If accompaniments are desired for these, they may be obtained in the Accompaniment Edition of *"The Silver Book."*

Recommended Phonograph Records

These three records were made especially for users of "The Silver Book" and are highly recommended:

V. 24539
- Airplane
- Autumn Leaves Are Falling
- Bobby Shafto
- Chinese Vegetable Man
- Dandelions
- Elfin Balloon
- Flowers' Message
- Goldenrod Is Waving
- He Didn't Think
- Lazy Robin
- Man in the Moon
- Merry Gardener
- Pussy Willows
- Thankful Song
- Wind

V. 24540
- Bonny Scotsmen
- Canoeing
- Children of Tyrol
- Daffodils
- Farewell, Spanish Ladies
- Feasting By the Ocean
- In Finland
- Island Song
- Stormy Sail
- To the Fringed Gentian
- Troika

V. 24541
- Bring a Torch, Jeanette, Isabella
- Carillon
- Come, Follow
- Conchita
- Lullaby
- Passing By
- Patient Stars
- Silver Book Theme Song
- Taps
- There Is My Home

Vocal records mentioned in the text and in the daily lesson plans in addition to those in the above group:

- V. 19830 Frog He Would A-Wooing Go—and others
- V. 19891 Windmill—and others
- V. 20214 Jolly Is the Miller—and others
- V. 20432 I See You—and others
- V. 20450 Wind the Bobbin (Shoemakers' Dance)—and others
- V. 20737 Cradle Song (Brahms' Lullaby)—and others
- V. 20739 Blacksmith
- V. 20743 There Are Many Flags in Many Lands
- V. 20744 To Italy (My Banjo)—and others
- V. 20806 Mulberry Bush
- V. 21428 America and Star-Spangled Banner

- V. 21618 Bow, Wow, Wow!—and others
- V. 21620 Dancing Lesson—and others
- V. 21751 Blow the Man Down—and others
- V. 21950 Old Folks at Home
- V. 22082 All Through the Night—Auld Lang Syne—and others
- V. 22083 America, the Beautiful—Columbia, the Gem of the Ocean—and others
- V. 22358 Over the River and Through the Wood
- V. 22617 Are You Sleeping, Brother John?—and others
- V. 22626 When Morning Gilds the Skies—and others

- V. 24241 Lightly Row—and others
- V. 24243 It Came Upon the Midnight Clear—O Come, All Ye Faithful—Silent Night—and others
- V. 24271 Home on the Range—Old Black Joe—and others
- V. 24273 Stars of the Summer Night—and others
- V. 24533 My Little Pony—and others
- V. 24534 Ten Little Indians—and others
- V. 24536 Sleepy Fishes—and others
- V. 35788 Christmas Hymns and Carols
- V. 35946 Christmas Hymns and Carols

Instrumental records mentioned in the text and in the daily lesson plans:

- C. 2720D Teddy Bears' Picnic
- V. 7021 Sorcerer's Apprentice
- V. 9271 Till Eulenspiegel, Pts. 1 & 2
- V. 9272 Till Eulenspiegel, Pts. 3 & 4
- V. 20079 Tarantelle — Elfin Dance—and others
- V. 20153 Of a Tailor and a Bear—and others
- V. 20158 Happy Farmer—and others
- V. 20169 Summer-Night's Dream (Amaryllis)—and others
- V. 20174 Sweet and Low—Cradle Song (Brahms' Lullaby)—and others
- V. 20350 Fundamental Rhythms, Nos. 1 & 2
- V. 20351 Fundamental Rhythms, Nos. 3 & 4
- V. 20399 March of the Tin Soldiers
- V. 20400 Tenth Regiment March—and others

- V. 20522 Instruments of the Orchestra—Strings and Woodwinds
- V. 20523 Instruments of the Orchestra—Brass and Percussion
- V. 20526 Rhythm Medley, Nos. 1 & 2
- V. 20606 Overture to William Tell (At Dawn, The Storm)
- V. 20802 Persephone's Return (Country Gardens)
- V. 20993 First Noel—and others
- V. 21449 Narcissus
- V. 21936 Now the Day Is Over
- V. 22013 Hail Columbia—and others
- V. 22166 Night and Day (Excerpt from "Ninth Symphony")—April's Wand (Londonderry Air)—and others

- V. 22168 Rhythms for Children
- V. 22175 / V. 22176 Hansel and Gretel—Selections from
- V. 22178 Twinkle, Twinkle, Little Star (The Question — Alphabet Song)—Bridge of Avignon—and others
- V. 22759 A-Hunting We Will Go—and others
- V. 22765 Nocturne (from Midsummer Night's Dream)—and others
- V. 24776 March of the Priests—and others
- V. 35785 Songs of Our Native Birds, Nos. 1 & 2
- V. 35792 In a Clock Store and Hunt in the Black Forest

Records recommended for music appreciation but not specifically named in the text or lesson plans:

- V. 1143 Swan and Moment Musical
- V. 6694 Lohengrin (Elsa's Dream, Elizabeth's Prayer)
- V. 6791 Lohengrin (Prelude—Pts. 1 & 2)
- V. 6904 Lohengrin (Swan Song, In Distant Lands)
- V. 7386 Lohengrin (Prelude to Act 3)
- V. 9005 Lohengrin (Prelude, Bridal Chorus)
- V. 9017 Lohengrin (Procession to the Cathedral)
- V. 7436 Hansel and Gretel (Overture)
- V. 19926 Melodies for Children

- V. 20011 Barcarolle
- V. 20395 Songs for Children
- V. 20525 Hungarian Fantasie and Whirlwind
- V. 20618 Daffodil Lady—and others
- V. 20801 Celeste Aïda—and others
- V. 22098 Children's Overture—Quilter, Pts. 1 & 2
- V. 22099 Children's Overture—Quilter, Pts. 3 & 4
- V. 22160 Cradle Song—Brahms (Vocal)—and others

- V. 22993 Cradle Song — Brahms (Instrumental)
- V. 22167 Music Box and Gavotte in F Major
- V. 24654 Andante "Surprise Symphony"—and others
- V. 24775 Tannhauser (Festival March)—and others
- V. 24782 Song of the Volga Boatman—and others
- V. 24783 Chant of the Snake Dancers—and others
- V. 35833 Dance of the Hours, Pts. 1 and 2

V.—Victor Record.   C.—Columbia Record.

Autumn Leaves

C.L.P.
KEY OF D   *Briskly*   C.L.P.

Down came the Au - tumn leaves, Whirl - ing a - round,
Do   ti   la   sol   fa   mi,   Fa   mi   re   do

Red, gold - en, yel - low, They cov - er the ground.
Do   ti   la   sol   fa,   Mi   fa   mi   re   do.

In September

C.L.P.
KEY OF E   GERMAN FOLK TUNE

Gaily

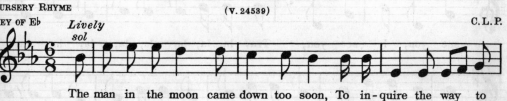

In gay Sep-tem-ber weath-er, The red and brown leaves, too,
Sol   do sol mi   do   sol sol,   Sol   do sol mi   do   re,

Go gai - ly float - ing, drift - ing down-ward, Leaves of love - ly hue.
Sol fa fa mi re sol   mi mi re do mi,   Re   fa   ti   re   do

The Man in the Moon

NURSERY RHYME   (V. 24539)
KEY OF E♭   *Lively*   C.L.P.
            sol

The man in the moon came down too soon, To in-quire the way to

Nor-wich; He went by the south and burnt his mouth, Eat-ing froz-en por-ridge.
Pronounced Nŏr-rĭj.

Wind the Bobbin

4

(V. 20450)

DANISH FOLK DANCE
OR SINGING GAME

Lively

Wind, wind, wind the bob-bin, Wind, wind, wind the bob-bin,

Pull, pull, and tap, tap, tap, Now we'll sew the right shoe O! Then we'll

stitch the left just so. Wind, wind, wind the bob-bin,

Wind, wind, wind the bob-bin, Pull, pull, and tap, tap, tap.

I See You

5

KEY OF G

(V. 20432)

SWEDISH FOLK DANCE
OR SINGING GAME

Gaily

I see you, I see you, Tra, la, la, la, la, la, la, la, la; I

see you, I see you, Tra, la, la, la, la, la, la, la, la;

If I see you and you see me, Then I take you and you take me; If

you see me and I see you, Then you take me and I take you.

The Dancing Lesson

6

(V. 21620)

KEY OF F

FOLK DANCE OR SINGING GAME
Sung in "HANSEL AND GRETEL"
ENGLEBERT HUMPERDINCK

Lively

GIRLS

Broth-er come and dance with me, Both my hands I'm off'ring thee;

This way first, that way now, Then a court-'sy and a bow, La, la, la,

p

BOYS

mf

la, la, la, la, la, la, la, la. Dance would I if I knew how, When to turn and

cresc

when to bow; Tell me what I ought to do, So I can dance the steps with you.

BOYS AND GIRLS

With your feet go tap, tap, tap, With your hands go clap, clap, clap;

cresc

This way first, that way now, Then a court-'sy and a bow.

Bow, Wow, Wow!

7

NURSERY RHYME
KEY OF G

(V. 21618)

AMERICAN SINGING GAME

Lively

do

Bow, wow, wow! Whose dog art thou?

Lit-tle Tom-my Tink-er's dog, Bow, wow, wow!

-103-

8

Jolly Is the Miller

(V. 20214)

KEY OF Ab   OLD ENGLISH FOLK GAME

Joyously

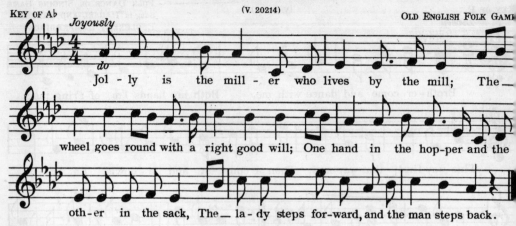

Jol-ly is the mill-er who lives by the mill; The
wheel goes round with a right good will; One hand in the hop-per and the
oth-er in the sack, The la-dy steps for-ward, and the man steps back.

9

Captain Hook

An Episode from "Peter Pan"

A Third Grade Poem
Adapted by ETHEL W. KILNER

KEY OF F MINOR   ROUMANIAN FOLK TUNE

Mischievously

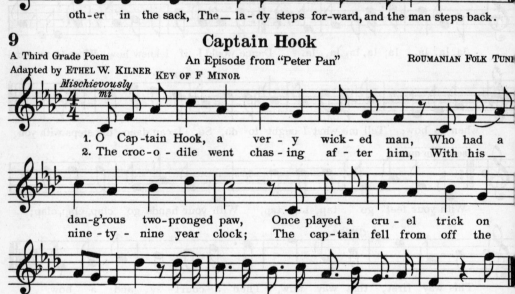

1. O Cap-tain Hook, a ver-y wick-ed man, Who had a
2. The croc-o-dile went chas-ing af-ter him, With his

dan-g'rous two-pronged paw, Once played a cru-el trick on
nine-ty-nine year clock; The cap-tain fell from off the

Pe-ter Pan, And laughed,"Haw, haw, haw, haw, haw, haw, haw, haw!"
pi-rate ship, With a yell and then an aw-ful, aw-ful plop, haw!

10

The Airplane

(V. 24589)

C.L.P.   C.L.P.

KEY OF G

Smoothly

Z-o-o-m, The air-plane is sing-ing As on-ward it goes wing-ing,
Near fleec-y clouds that soft-ly lie, Guard-ing high-ways of the sky.

(V. 20806)

ENGLISH NURSERY TUNE

KEY OF Ab

Gaily   do

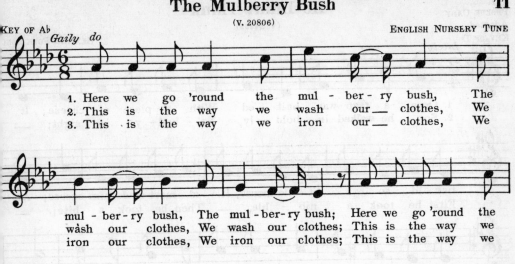

1. Here we go 'round the mul - ber - ry bush, The
2. This is the way we wash our __ clothes, We
3. This is the way we iron our __ clothes, We

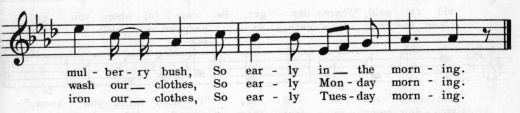

mul - ber - ry bush, The mul - ber - ry bush; Here we go 'round the
wash our clothes, We wash our clothes; This is the way we
iron our clothes, We iron our clothes; This is the way we

mul - ber - ry bush, So ear - ly in __ the morn - ing.
wash our __ clothes, So ear - ly Mon - day morn - ing.
iron our __ clothes, So ear - ly Tues - day morn - ing.

4. This is the way we scrub the floor, etc.   So early Wednesday morning.
5. This is the way we mend our clothes, etc.   So early Thursday morning.
6. This is the way we sweep the floor, etc.   So early Friday morning.
7. This is the way we bake our bread, etc.   So early Saturday morning.
8. This is the way we go to church, etc.   So early Sunday morning.

Pussy Willows

12

M.H.H.

(V. 24539)

MARY H. HOWLISTON

KEY OF Eb

Smoothly

mp

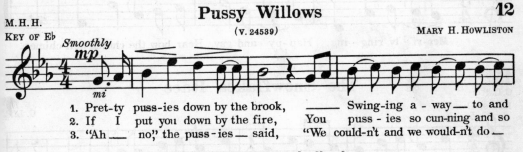

mi

1. Pret-ty puss-ies down by the brook, ____ Swing-ing a - way __ to and
2. If I put you down by the fire, You puss - ies so cun-ning and so
3. "Ah __ no" the puss-ies __ said, "We could-n't and we would-n't do __

gradually slower

fro. On the bend-ing wil-low boughs Like puss-y cats all in a row.
shy, I __ won - der if you'd turn In-to puss-y cats by and by?
that. We be-long to the fair-y folk. And __ we __ are their puss-y __ cats."

13

PHOEBE CARY
Adapted

KEY OF D

He Didn't Think
(V. 24539)

GERMAN FOLK SONG

Lively

1. Once a trap was bait - ed With a piece of cheese; It
2. So he walked in bold - ly, No - bod - y in sight; —

tick - l'd so a lit - tle mouse, It al - most made him sneeze; An
First he took a nib - ble, — Then he took a bite;

old rat said, "There's dan - ger, Be care - ful where you go!"
Close the trap to - geth - er — Snapped as quick as wink,

rit.

"Non - sense!" said the oth - er, "I don't think you know."
Catch - ing mous - ie fast there, 'Cause he did - n't think.

14

HAZEL LOUISE BROWN

KEY OF G

The Church Bell

C. L. P.

Merrily

Mer - ri - ly ring - ing, Hap - py and gay, Hear how the church bell chimes.

15

C.L.P.

KEY OF C

The Snowflakes' Race

C. L. P.

Lively

Gay lit - tle snow flakes flut' - ring down: Fall in a heap on the froz - en ground. A-

long comes the wind at a ter - ri - ble pace, Call - ing all the snowflakes to come for a race.

(V. 22178)

TRANSLATED FROM THE FRENCH
Adapted by ANN TRIMINGHAM

FRENCH FOLK SONG

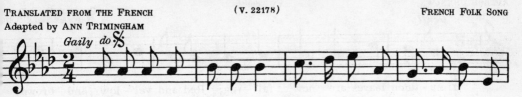

On the bridge of A - vi - gnon, All are danc-ing; all are danc-ing;

On the bridge of A - vi - gnon, All are danc-ing in a ring.

1. Gen - tle - men bow this way, Then a - gain bow that way.
2. La - dies curt - sy this way, Then all curt - sy that way.
3. Stal - wart boys step this way, Then a - gain step that way.
4. Dain - ty girls trip this way, Then a - gain trip that way.

* Pronounced, à́-vḗ-nyon.

A-Hunting We Will Go 17

(V. 22759)

KEY OF Ab

OLD ENGLISH SINGING GAME

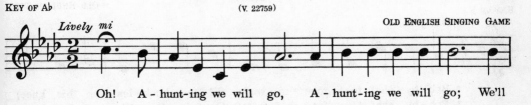

Oh! A - hunt-ing we will go, A - hunt-ing we will go; We'll

catch a lit - tle fox, And put him in a box, And then we'll let him go.

18

Autumn Leaves Are Falling
(V. 24539)

AUTHOR UNKNOWN
KEY OF F

GERMAN FOLK TUNE

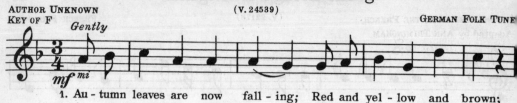

Gently

1. Au - tumn leaves are now fall - ing; Red and yel - low and brown;
2. Au - tumn leaves from the tree tops Flut - ter down to the ground,
3. Au - tumn leaves when they're tired,—— In a soft hud - dled heap,

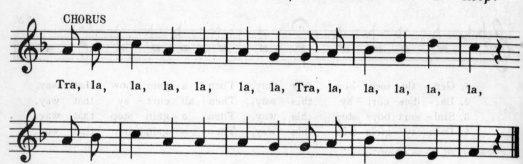

Au - tumn leaves are now fall - ing, See them flut - ter - ing down.
When the wind blows his trump - et, They go whirl - ing a - round.
At the foot of the old tree, Soon will fall fast a - sleep.

CHORUS

Tra, la, la, la, la, la, la, Tra, la, la, la, la, la,

Tra, la, la, la, la, la, la, Tra, la, la, la, la, la.

19

Bobby Shafto
(V. 24539)

MOTHER GOOSE
KEY OF F

OLD ENGLISH TUNE

Blithely

mi

1. Bob - by Shaf - to's gone to sea! Sil - ver buck - les on his knee;
2. Bob - by Shaf - to's fat and fair, Comb - ing down his yel - low hair;

He'll come back and mar - ry me,—— Pret - ty Bob - by Shaf - to!
He's my love for - ev - er - more,— Pret - ty Bob - by Shaf - to!

MAUDE M. GRANT

C. L. P.

KEY OF E

Briskly

Blow, old March wind, blow, blow, blow! Make the arms of the

wind - mill go,__ Flut - ter the clothes on the clothes-line high,

Blow our kites to the far blue sky. Push the sail - boats

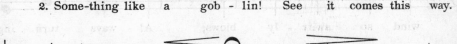

o - ver the deep, And wak - en the buds from their win - ter sleep.

Reprinted from March 1933 issue of *The Instructor*. Courtesy F. A. Owen Publishing Co.

Jack-O'-Lantern Gay 21

Adapted by C.L.P.

KEY OF Ab

Not too fast

1. Oh, look out the win - dow! What is that I see?
2. Some-thing like a gob - lin! See it comes this way.

I see such an aw - ful thing A - look - ing in at me.
Oh, I know now what it is! A jack-o' - lan - tern gay.

22 My Little Pony

HAHN

KEY OF G

(V. 24533)

GERMAN FOLK SONG

Lively

1. Hop, hop, hop! Go, and nev-er stop; Where it's smooth and where it's ston-y, Trot a-long, my lit-tle po-ny; Go, and nev-er stop; Hop, hop, hop, hop, hop!
2. Hey, hey, hey! Go a-long, I say! Do not kick and nev-er stum-ble, Do not tire and nev-er grum-ble; Go a-long, I say; Hey, hey, hey, hey, hey!
3. Jump, jump, jump! Do not hit that stump! Nev-er will I cease to ride you, Till I far-ther yet have tried you; Shun, I say, that stump. Jump, jump, jump, jump, jump!

23 The Windmill

FRIEDRICH FROEBEL

KEY OF Eb

(V. 19891)

GERMAN FOLK SONG

Not too fast

See the wind-mill how it goes, While the wind so swift-ly blows; Al-ways turn-ing round and round, Nev-er i-dle is it found.

Twinkle, Twinkle, Little Star

(V. 22178—The Question—Alphabet Song)

JANE TAYLOR
KEY OF G

WOLFGANG MOZART

Not too slowly

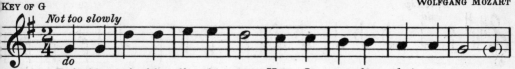

do

1. Twin-kle, twin-kle, lit-tle star; How I won-der what you are,
2. When the blaz-ing sun is gone, When he noth-ing shines up-on,
3. Then the trav'l-er in the dark Thanks you for your ti-ny spark; He
4. In the dark blue sky you keep, While you thro' my win-dow peep,

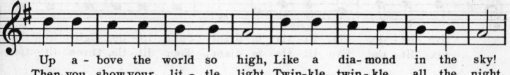

Up a-bove the world so high, Like a dia-mond in the sky!
Then you show your lit-tle light, Twin-kle, twin-kle, all the night.
could not see which way to go, If you did not twin-kle so.
And you nev-er shut your eye, Till the sun is in the sky.

Twin-kle, twin-kle, lit-tle star, How I won-der what you are.

The Dandelions

(V. 24539)

C. L. P.
KEY OF Eb

CLELLA LESTER PERKINS

Lively

mf mi

1. Sau-cy lit-tle dan-de-li-ons With your gold-en sheen;
2. Shall I snip your bright heads off Ere the pass-ing day
3. If I do not mow you down, What will hap-pen, pray?

You are yel-low pol-ka dots On a field of green.
Turns your shin-ing gold-en locks In-to sil-v'ry gray?
Naugh-ty South Wind in his play Will blow you far a-way.

Ten Little Indians

(V. 24534)

OLD SONG

Briskly

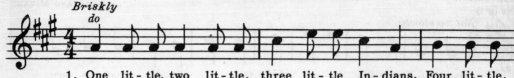

1. One lit-tle, two lit-tle, three lit-tle In-dians, Four lit-tle,
2. Ten lit-tle, nine lit-tle, eight lit-tle In-dians, Sev'n lit-tle,

five lit-tle, six lit-tle In-dians, Sev'n lit-tle, eight lit-tle,
six lit-tle, five lit-tle In-dians, Four lit-tle, three lit-tle,

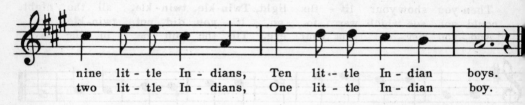

nine lit-tle In-dians, Ten lit-tle In-dian boys.
two lit-tle In-dians, One lit-tle In-dian boy.

Ten Little Indians

KEY OF F

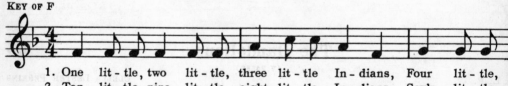

1. One lit-tle, two lit-tle, three lit-tle In-dians, Four lit-tle,
2. Ten lit-tle, nine lit-tle, eight lit-tle In-dians, Sev'n lit-tle,

five lit-tle, six lit-tle In-dians, Sev'n lit-tle, eight lit-tle,
six lit-tle, five lit-tle In-dians, Four lit-tle, three lit-tle,

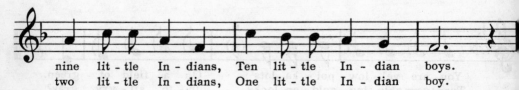

nine lit-tle In-dians, Ten lit-tle In-dian boys.
two lit-tle In-dians, One lit-tle In-dian boy.

28

Twenty Froggies Went to School

GEORGE COOPER
KEY OF G

Composer Unknown

Merrily

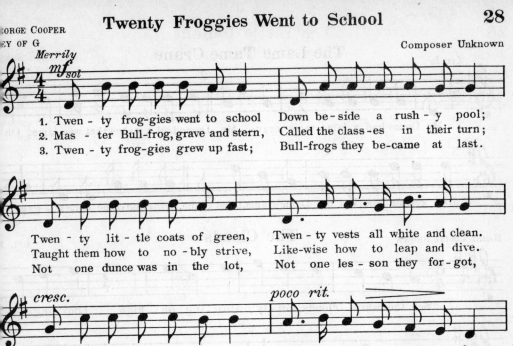

1. Twen - ty frog-gies went to school | Down be - side a rush - y pool;
2. Mas - ter Bull-frog, grave and stern, | Called the class-es in their turn;
3. Twen - ty frog-gies grew up fast; | Bull-frogs they be-came at last.

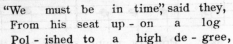

Twen - ty lit - tle coats of green, | Twen - ty vests all white and clean.
Taught them how to no - bly strive, | Like-wise how to leap and dive.
Not one dunce was in the lot, | Not one les - son they for - got,

cresc. *poco rit.*

"We must be in time," said they, | "First we stud - y, then we play;
From his seat up - on a log | Taught them how to say, "Ker - chog!"
Pol - ished to a high de - gree, | As each frog-gie ought to be.

a tempo *rit.*

That is how we keep the rule, | When we frog-gies go to school."
Like - wise how to dodge a blow | From the sticks which bad boys throw.
Now they sit on oth - er logs, | Teach-ing oth - er lit - tle frogs.

The Cuckoo

29

KEY OF F

GERMAN FOLK SONG

Gaily

1. Cuck - oo! | Cuck - oo! | Don't try to hide from me;
2. Cuck - oo! | Cuck - oo! | It's such an eas - y song;

Cuck - oo! | Cuck - oo! | I see you in the tree.
Cuck - oo! | Cuck - oo! | It's hard to get it wrong.

The Lame Tame Crane

Lively

My Dame had a lame tame crane, My Dame had a crane that was lame, Oh
pray gen-tle Jane; Let my Dame's lame, tame crane, Drink and come home a - gain.

HAZEL LOUISE BROWN

The Clouds

C. L. B.

See the white clouds soft-ly float-ing on high   Look-ing so
bright in the blue of the sky;   Pret-ty white clouds are the
soft lit-tle beds;   Where the Sun fair-ies, lay their sleep-y heads.

Three Blind Mice

(Round)

Three blind mice, — Three blind mice, — See how they run, — See how they
run! They all ran af-ter the farm-er's wife, She cut off their tails with a
carv-ing knife; Did ev-er you see such a thing in your life, As three blind mice?

Jolly Old St. Nicholas

32

Adapted by C. L. P.

KEY OF Ab

OLD SONG

1. Jol - ly old St. Nich - o - las, Lean your ear this way,
2. When the clock is strik - ing twelve, When I'm fast a - sleep,
3. John - ny wants a pair of skates, Su - sy wants a sled;

Don't you tell a sin - gle soul, What I'm going to say;
Down the chim - ney broad and black, With your pack you'll creep;
Nel - ly wants a pic - ture book Yel - low, blue, and red;

Christ-mas eve is com - ing soon, Now you dear old man,
Soon you'll find the stock-ings there Hang-ing in a row,
Now I think I'll leave to you What to give the rest;

Whis - per what you'll bring to me, Soft - ly as you can.
Mine will be the short - est one, Mend - ed at the toe.
Choose for me, dear San - ta Claus, You will know the best.

Sail Swift, White Ship

HAZEL LOUISE BROWN

C. L. P.

KEY OF C

Sail swift, white ship, a - cross the foam, Sail fast o - ver the rest-less sea,

And take my mes-sage safe to one Who will be wait - ing to hear from me.

A Thankful Song

(V. 24539)

AUTHOR UNKNOWN
KEY OF D

CLELLA LESTER PERKIN[S]

We thank you for the flow'rs so sweet, We thank you for the food we eat, We thank you for the birds that sing, We thank you, God, for ev-'ry-thing.

Reprinted from April 1933 issue of CHILD LIFE. Courtesy Rand McNally & Co., Publishers.

35

The Bells

C. L. P.

KEY OF Eb

FRENCH FOLK TUN[E]

All the bells are gai-ly ring-ing, Bing, bong, bing, bong; Call-ing us to hear them sing-ing, Bing, bing, bong.

36

The Grocer and the Housewife

C.L.P.

KEY OF E

Composer Unknown

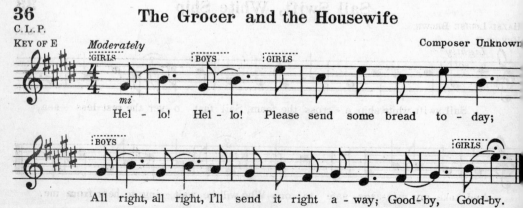

GIRLS BOYS GIRLS

Hel-lo! Hel-lo! Please send some bread to-day;

BOYS GIRLS

All right, all right, I'll send it right a-way; Good-by, Good-by.

- 116 -

KEY OF Eb   OLD SONG

Gaily

A sweet lit - tle rob - in one morn - ing in Spring,

Flew in - to the or - chard and stopped there to sing;

His heart was so light and his song was so gay,

I asked him what song he was sing - ing to - day.

"Ti - ri - lee - lee, Ti - ri - lee - lee; No - bod - y knows but my

mate and me;" "Ti - ri - lee - lee, Ti - ri -

lee - lee; Up in the nest with our lit - tle birds three."

The Chinese Vegetable Man

AGNES E. PETERSON

KEY OF G

(V. 24539)

LOUIS WOODSON CURTIS

Ching, Ching, Chi-na-man, jog-ging down the street, Bas-kets on his shoul-ders,

flap-ping shoes on feet; "Cal-lots, let-tuce, lad - ish," can't you hear him sing?

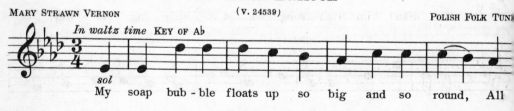

Please to stop at our house, smil-ing Mis-ter Ching. _____

★ *Pidgin English for "Carrots, lettuce, radish," in imitation of the supposed inability of the Chinese to speak the letter "r".*

The Elfin Balloon

MARY STRAWN VERNON

(V. 24539)

POLISH FOLK TUNE

My soap bub - ble floats up so big and so round, All

tint - ed with rain - bow light,— That some el - fin air-man is

sure to hop in And take off for a strat - o - sphere flight. —

44

The Wind
(v. 24539)

TRADITIONAL
KEY OF G

ENGLISH FOLK SONG

Lightly

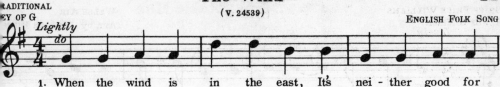

1. When the wind is in the east, It's nei - ther good for
2. When the wind is in the west, The corn and clo - ver
3. When the jol - ly North Wind blows, It brings the cold and
4. When the gen - tle South Wind blows, The flow'rs their pet - als

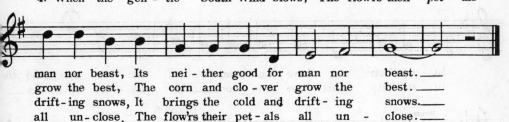

man nor beast, Its nei - ther good for man nor beast.____
grow the best, The corn and clo - ver grow the best.____
drift - ing snows, It brings the cold and drift - ing snows.____
all un - close, The flow'rs their pet - als all un - close.____

Swinging

45

HAZEL LOUISE BROWN
KEY OF A

C. L. P.

Gracefully

Up, up high - er, see us go! Swing high; swing high; then swing low;
Do do re re mi fa sol, Sol mi sol mi fa mi re.

Soft - ly, soft - ly, to and fro; Till we're swing - ing ver - y slow.
Re re mi mi fa sol la sol la sol fa mi re do.

The Swallows

KEY OF G

OLD SONG

Smoothly

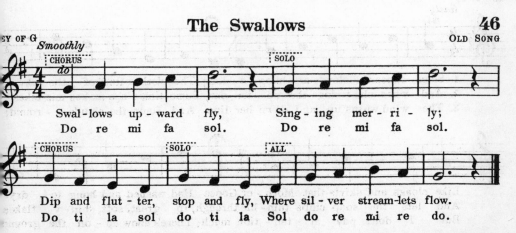

CHORUS

Swal - lows up - ward fly,
Do re mi fa sol.

SOLO

Sing - ing mer - ri - ly;
Do re mi fa sol.

CHORUS

Dip and flut - ter,
Do ti la sol

SOLO

stop and fly,
do ti la

ALL

Where sil - ver stream-lets flow.
Sol do re mi re do.

Lazy Robin

GRIFF PRICE WILLIAMS
KEY OF G MINOR

WELSH AIR
Arr. by WILLIAM HUGH[

Lively

1. I have a beau-ti-ful lit-tle hut, A lit-tle hut, a
2. Just ope the door a lit-tle bit, A lit-tle bit, a

lit-tle hut; I have a beau-ti-ful lit-tle hut And the
lit-tle bit; Just ope the door a lit-tle bit So

CHORUS

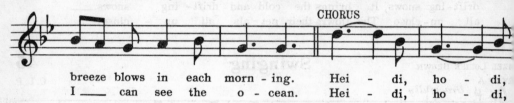

breeze blows in each morn-ing. Hei-di, ho-di,
I can see the o-cean. Hei-di, ho-di,

hei-di, hei-di, ho! And the breeze blows in each morn-ing.
hei-di, hei-di, ho! So I can see the o-cean.

First Snow

ELEANOR JEWETT
KEY OF F

CLELLA LESTER PERKI[

Gaily

1. Some-times the clouds are hung a-long The clothes-line of the sky,
2. And when she wrings the wa-ter out, Some-times she makes mis-takes
3. The wind whips up and down her line, And flaps the clouds a-round;

Like cloaks and skirts that Moth-er Goose Had washed and hung to dry.
And lets the soap chips tum-ble through, In great, soft, shin-y flakes
But I don't pay at-ten-tion much; There's snow up-on the ground

At Sea

M. S. V.

From "CHIMES OF NORMANDY"
JEAN ROBERT PLANQUETTE

In swinging rhythm

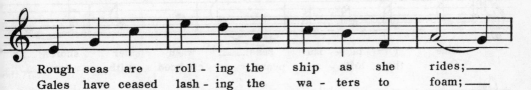

1. Wild winds are blow - ing, white caps are show - ing,
2. Ham - mocks are swing - ing, Jack Tars are sing - ing,

Rough seas are roll - ing the ship as she rides; —
Gales have ceased lash - ing the wa - ters to foam; —

Wrapped in great bil - lows, wave crests her pil - lows,
Qui - et de - scends now, star - ry sky bends now

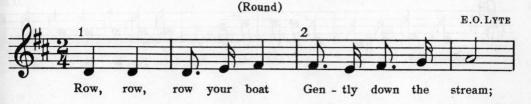

Brave - ly she sails on, what - ev - er be - tides.
Ov - er the sail - or lads dream - ing of home.

Row, Row, Row Your Boat
(Round)

E. O. LYTE

Row, row, row your boat Gen - tly down the stream;

Mer - ri - ly, mer - ri - ly, mer - ri - ly, mer - ri - ly, Life is but a dream.

51 To Italy

Translated and adapted by M.S.V.

(V. 20744 — My Banjo)

ITALIAN FOLK SONG

Cantabile

Blue I - tal - ian skies arch high a - bove her,
Sun - set col - ors glow with match - less ra - diance,

Blue I - tal - ian seas____ wash her shores;____
On the loft - y peaks en - crowned with snow;____

Blue I - tal - ian lakes____ mir - ror her moun - tains,
Ev - 'ning air is sweet with flow'r-scent - ed fra - grance,

Fine

Through her days of warm sun - shine pours.
Soft, cool night - winds gen - tly blow.

Hark! the gay gui - tars strum-ming through the val - leys,

D. C.

Sounds of hap - py songs and danc - ing feet. Tra, la, la, la, la!

52 The Boys of the Zuider Zee

M.S.V.

FOLK TUNE OF
THE NETHERLANDS

Leggiero

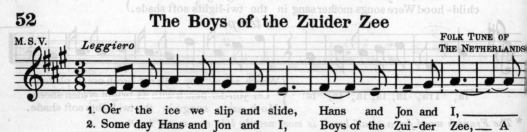

1. O'er the ice we slip and slide, Hans and Jon and I,____
2. Some day Hans and Jon and I, Boys of the Zui - der Zee,____ A

Bet - tje★ comes with dip and glide, Skat- ing swift-ly by; _____
big sea-plane will learn to fly, And sail far out to sea;___ Then

Swift-ly as a wild bird flies, Or white cloud rac - es through the skies,
back once more a-cross the Main, To Am-ster- dam we'll fly a- gain, And

Sure-ly she will win the prize, Bet - tje, qui -et and shy. ___
Bet - tje will be glad to see The boys of the Zui - der Zee. ___

★ *Bettje is pronounced Betty.*

In Finland

53

Adapted by M.S.V.   (v. 24540)   FINNISH FOLK TUNE

Andantino

1. Far o'er the sea in the depths of the wild wood, Hid - den a-
2. Blue are the skies arch-ing wide o'er the dark pine, Gild - ed the
3. Mu - sic sounds al - ways in that leaf - y wild-wood, Bird notes and

way in a dim for-est glade, Still stands the hut★,__ the home of my
light sift-ing down thro' the green; Blue are the waves dash-ing high in the
deep tones by toss - ing waves made; Yet sweet-est of all of the sounds of my

piu mosso

child - hood, Where as a boy with my broth ers I played. ⎫
sun - shine, On yon-der beach with its bright gold-en sheen. ⎬ Tra, la, la, la, la,
child- hood Were songs mother sang in the twi-light's soft shade. ⎭

a tempo

la, Tra, la, la, la, la, la! ⎧ Where as a boy with my broth ers I played.
                       ⎨ On yon-der beach with its bright golden sheen.
                       ⎩ Moth-er's songs in the twi-light's soft shade.

★ *The Finnish word for a small house is most nearly like our word "hut."*

-123-

58

A Frog He Would A-Wooing Go

Author Unknown

OLD ENGLISH SONG

Giocoso

1. A frog he would a - woo-ing go, m - m, m - m, A frog he would a -
2. He rode right to Miss Mous-ie's den, m - m, m - m, He rode right to Miss
3. "Yes, kind Sir Frog, I sit to spin," m - m, m - m, "Yes, kind Sir Frog, I
4. He said, "My dear I've come to see," m - m, m - m, He said, "My dear I've
5. "I don't know what to say to that," m - m, m - m, "I don't know what to
6. When Un-cle Rat came rid-ing home, m - m, m - m, When Un-cle Rat came
7. "A fine young gentleman has been here," m - m, m - m, "A fine young gentleman
8. So Un-cle Rat he rode to town, m - m, m - m, So Un-cle Rat he
9. The frog and mouse they went to France, m-m, m - m, The frog and mouse they

woo-ing go, ___ Wheth-er his moth-er would let him or no, m - m, m - m.
Mous-ie's den, Said he, "Miss Mous-ie are you with-in?" m - m, m - m.
sit to spin,_ Pray Mis-ter Frog-gie won't you walk in?" m - m, m - m.
come to see, If you, Miss Mous-ie, will mar - ry me?" m - m, m - m.
say to that, Till I ___ can see ___ my Un-cle Rat." m - m, m - m.
rid - ing home, Said he, "Who's been here since I've been gone?" m - m, m - m.
has been here, Who wants to mar-ry me it is clear." m - m, m - m.
rode to town, And bought his niece_ a wed-ding gown. m - m, m - m.
went to France, And that is the end ___ of my ro-mance. m - m, m - m.

59

The Happy Farmer

ROBERT SCHUMANN

Giojoso

1. Oh what can with our flow - 'ry plains com-pare, In
2. The bright green fields, the beau-teous gold - en corn, The
3. We sing sweet songs and join the mer - ry dance, And

all their match-less beau-ty that's so bright and fair? What gild - ed halls can
birds so sweet-ly sing-ing in the ear - ly morn, Make bright our task and
joy - ful-ness and pleas-ure do each heart en-trance, Till night's dark man - tle

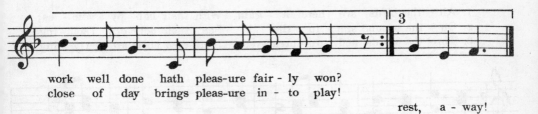

ri - val na-ture's bow'rs, 'Neath which we gai-ly pass a-way the eve-ning hours, When
cheer-'ly through the day, Do pass on swift-ly fleet-ing wings the hours a-way, Till
clos-ing o - ver day, Bids each with light-some heart a-way to

work well done hath pleas-ure fair - ly won?
close of day brings pleas-ure in - to play!

rest, a - way!

Are You Sleeping, Brother John? 60
(Christmas Bells)

(V. 22617)

OLD FRENCH ROUND

1. Are you sleep - ing, Are you sleep - ing,
2. Christ - mas bells, ____ Christ - mas bells, ____

Broth - er John, Broth - er John?
Hear them ring! Hear them ring!

Morn - ning bells are ring - ing, Morn - ning bells are
From the bel - fry stee - ple, From the bel - fry

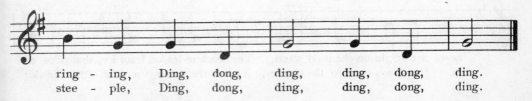

ring - ing, Ding, dong, ding, ding, dong, ding.
stee - ple, Ding, dong, ding, ding, dong, ding.

-125-

All the Birds Are Here Again

84

JANE B. WALTERS

BOHEMIAN FOLK SONG

Allegretto

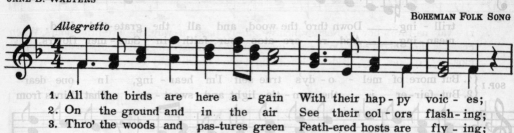

1. All the birds are here a - gain With their hap - py voic - es;
2. On the ground and in the air See their col - ors flash - ing;
3. Thro' the woods and pas-tures green Feath-ered hosts are fly - ing;

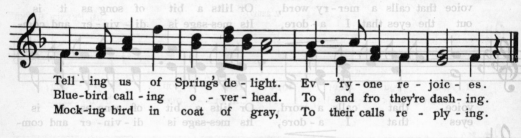

Nois - y spar-row, wren so bright, Chirp and sing from morn till night,
Rob - in dear, with breast of red, Scratch-ing in the gar - den bed,
Mead-ow lark with war - ble gay, Bob-white whis-tling all the day,

Tell - ing us of Spring's de - light. Ev - 'ry-one re - joic - es.
Blue-bird call - ing o - ver - head. To and fro they're dash - ing.
Mock-ing bird in coat of gray, To their calls re - ply - ing.

105

MYRTLE KOON CHERRYMAN
Adapted

April's Wand
(V. 22166)

LONDONDERRY AIR
Arr. by C. L. P.

Andante

1. There comes a sound to ev - 'ry heart so thrill - ing, When A-pril
2. There is a light that comes when Spring is green - ing; It quiv-ers

waves her bright en-chant-ed wand, The brook re-leased from ice, that goes a
on the grass-es, thro' the show'rs; It gives the earth a wist - ful, ten-der

trill - ing_____ Down thro' the wood, and all the grate - ful land.
mean - ing,_____ And re - cre - ates our faith in Sum - mer flow'rs.

SOP. I
1. But more of mel - o - dy's true self I'm hear - ing, In one dear
2. But fair - er is the gen - tle light and sweet - er, That shines from

SOP. II & ALTO
1. But more of mel - o - dy's true self hear - ing, In one dear
2. But fair - er is gen - tle light and sweet - er, That shines from

voice that calls a mer - ry word, Or lilts a bit of song as it is
out the eyes that I a - dore, Its mes - sage is di - vin - er and com-

voice that calls a word, Or lilts a bit of song as it is
eyes that I a - dore, Its mes - sage is di - vin - er and com-

near - ing, For it is mu - sic that my ver - y heart has stirred.
plet - er, And gives this hu - man life a rich - ness ev - er - more.

near - ing, For mu - sic my___ heart ___ has stirred.
plet - er, Gives life___ rich - ness ev - er - more.

117 Persephone's Return

A Gay Springtime Carol

JEAN STENHOUSE
Adapted by M.S.V.

(V.20802) — Country Garden

MORRIS DANCE
Arr. by M.S.V.

1. Warm winds are blow - ing, brooks all are flow - ing, Per-
2. Gar - d'ners are sow - ing, rak - ing or hoe - ing, Per-

seph - o - ne is back a - gain; Or-chards all a - bloom, __
seph - o - ne is back a - gain; All the birds are sing - ing,

scat - ter rich per - fume, __ Farm - ers at work with
joy - ous notes are ring - ing, Spring is the gay - est

right __ good cheer. So __ dance to the meas - ure,
time __ of year.

Now's the time for pleas-ure, Per-seph - o - ne once more is here.

118 Summer - Night's Dream

M.S.V.

(V. 20169) — Amarylis

OLD FRENCH GAVOTTE
Arr. by M.S.V.

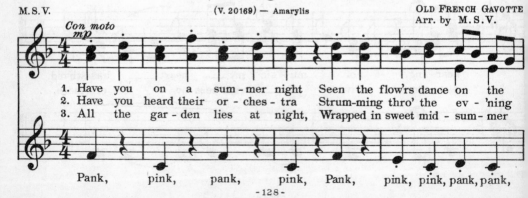

Con moto
mp

1. Have you on a sum - mer night Seen the flow'rs dance on the
2. Have you heard their or - ches - tra Strum - ming thro' the ev - 'ning
3. All the gar - den lies at night, Wrapped in sweet mid - sum - mer

Pank, pink, pank, pink, Pank, pink, pink, pank, pank,

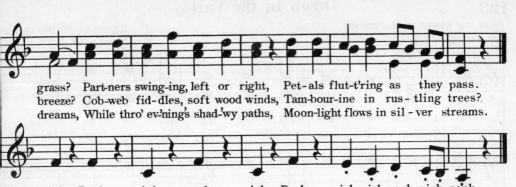

grass? Part-ners swing-ing, left or right, Pet-als flut-t'ring as they pass.
breeze? Cob-web fid-dles, soft wood winds, Tam-bour-ine in rus-tling trees?
dreams, While thro' ev'ning's shad-'wy paths, Moon-light flows in sil-ver streams.

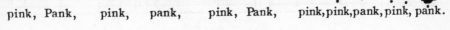

pink, Pank, pink, pank, pink, Pank, pink, pink, pank, pink, pank.

Cold's the Wind   55

Second Stanza
By C.L.P.

OLD ENGLISH SONG

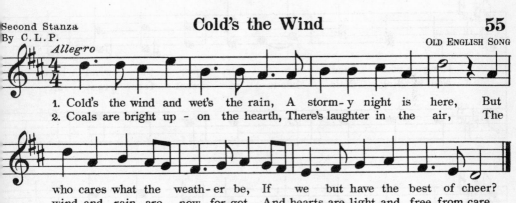

Allegro

1. Cold's the wind and wet's the rain, A storm-y night is here, But
2. Coals are bright up-on the hearth, There's laughter in the air, The

who cares what the weath-er be, If we but have the best of cheer?
wind and rain are now for-got, And hearts are light and free from care.

Bonny Scotsmen   64

C.L.P.

(v.24540)

OLD SCOTCH TUNE

Animato

1. A - wa', lads, a - wa'. A - wa', lads, a - wa'. Ye're
2. A - wa', lads, a - wa'. A - wa', lads, a - wa'. Ye'll

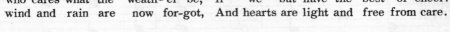

bon-ny Scots-men, strang and true, In tar-tan plaid so braw.
fol-low trump-et, pipe, and drum, What-ev-er may be-fa'.

This rhythmic figure (♪♪.) is called the "Scotch snap."

123   Down in the Valley

FROM THE KENTUCKY MOUNTAINS
Adapted by C. L. P.

KENTUCKY MOUNTAIN TUNE
Arr. by C.L.P.

Moderato

1. Down in the val - ley, the val - ley so low,
2. Ros - es are bloom - ing, bloom-ing so fair,

Hang your head o - ver, hear the wind blow,
Nod - ding their heads in sweet fra - grant air,

Hear the wind blow, dear, hear the wind blow,
Day - time brings sun - shine, night - time the dew,

Hang your head o - ver, hear the wind blow!
An - gels in heav - en know I love you.

Over the River and Through the Wood

LYDIA MARIA CHILD

COMPOSER UNKNOWN
Arr. by C. L. P.

Allegretto

1. O - ver the riv - er and thro' the wood, To grand-fa-ther's house we go; — The
2. O - ver the riv - er and thro' the wood, To have a first-rate play; Oh
3. O - ver the riv - er and thro' the wood, And straight thro' the barn-yard gate, We

horse knows the way to car-ry the sleigh, Thro' the white and drift-ed snow. —
hear the bells ring, — "Ting-a-ling-ling!" Hur - rah for Thanks-giv-ing Day. —
seem to go ex - treme - ly slow It — is — so hard to wait!

O - ver the riv - er and thro' the wood, Oh, how — the wind does blow! — It
O - ver the riv - er and thro' the wood, Trot fast — my dap - ple gray! Spring
O - ver the riv - er and thro' the wood, Now grand-moth-er's cap I spy! — Hur-

stings the toes, And bites the nose, As o - ver the ground we go. —
o-ver the ground, Like a hunt-ing hound! For this is Thanks-giv-ing Day. —
rah for the fun! Is the pud-ding done? Hur-rah for the pump-kin pie! —

Blow the Man Down

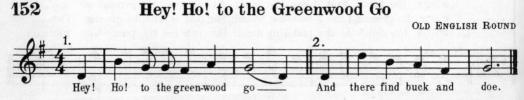

Hey! Ho! to the Greenwood Go

Home on the Range

(V. 24271)

COWBOY SONG
Arr. by C.L.P.

Animato

1. O,___ give me a home where the buf - fa - lo roam, Where the
2. How___ oft - en at night where the heav-en's are bright, With the
3. O,___ give me a land where the bright dia-mond sand, Flows___
4. Where the air is so pure, the___ zeph-yrs so free, The___
5. Oh, I love those wild flow'rs in this dear land of ours, The___

deer and the an - te - lope play.___ Where sel - dom is heard a dis -
lights from the glit - ter - ing stars.___ Have I stood there a - mazed and___
lei - sure-ly down the___ stream; Where the grace-ful white swan goes___
breez - es so balm - y and light,___ That I would not ex-change my___
cur - lew I love to hear scream, And I love the white rocks and the

cour - ag - ing word, And the skies are not cloud - y all day.___
asked as I gazed, If their glo - ry ex-ceeds that of ours.___
glid - ing a - long, Like a maid in a heav - en - ly dream.___
home on the range, For___ all of the cit - ies so bright.___
an - te - lope flocks, That___ graze on the moun-tain-tops green.___

REFRAIN

Home, home on the range, Where the deer and the an - te - lope play.___Where

sel - dom is heard a dis-cour-ag-ing word, And the skies are not cloud-y all day. ___

-133-

133 The Birds' Ball

OLD SONG
Arr. by C. L. P.

Lively

1. The Spring once said to the night-in-gale, "I
2. Soon they came from bush and tree
3. The cuck-oo and wren they danc'd for life, The
4. The wood-peck-er came from his hole in the tree, And
5. They danc'd all day till the sun was low, The

mean to give you birds a ball," "Pray, ma'am, ask the
Sing-ing sweet their songs of glee; Each one fresh from its
rav-en waltz'd with the yel-low-bird's wife; The awk-ward owl and the
bro't his bill to the com-pa-ny, For cher-ries ripe and
moth-er birds pre-pared to go; Then one and all, both

bird-ies all, The birds and bird-ies great and small."
co-sy nest, Each one dressed in its Sun-day best.
bash-ful jay, Wished each oth-er a "very good day."
ber-ries red, 'Twas a ver-y long bill, so the bird-ies said.
great and small, Flew to their nests from "the bird-ies ball."

CHORUS

Tra, la, la, la, la, Tra, la, la, la, la, Tra, la, la, la, la, Tra, la, la, la, la,

Tra, la, la, la, la, Tra, la, la, la, la, Tra, la, la, la, la, la, la, la, la.

★ *Basses divide*

-134-

There Are Many Flags in Many Lands

(V. 20743)

142

M. H. HOWLISTON

COMPOSER UNKNOWN
Arr. by M.S.V.

★ *Chorus may be sung in unison if desired.*

Old Black Joe
(v. 24271)

STEPHEN C. FOSTER

Poco adagio

1. Gone are the days when my heart was young and gay; __ Gone are my friends from the
2. Why do I weep when my heart should feel no pain? __ Why do I sigh that my
3. Where are the hearts once so hap-py and so free? The chil-dren so dear that I

cot-ton fields a-way; Gone from the earth to a bet-ter land I know,
friends come not a-gain? Griev-ing for forms now de-part-ed long a-go, I
held up-on my knee? Gone to the shore where my soul has long'd to go,

mf CHORUS *pp* *mf*

hear their gen-tle voic-es call-ing, "Old Black Joe!" I'm com-ing, I'm com-ing, For my

mf *pp* *pp* *poco rit.*

head is bend-ing low; I hear their gen-tle voic-es call-ing, "Old Black Joe!"

157

Stars of the Summer Night
HENRY W. LONGFELLOW
(v. 24273)

ISAAC B. WOODBURY

Andante

p *poco cresc.*

1. Stars of the sum-mer night, Far in yon az-ure deeps, Hide, hide your
2. Moon of the sum-mer night, Far down yon west-ern steeps, Sink, sink in
3. Dreams of the sum-mer night, Tell her, her lov-er keeps, Watch, while in

gold- en light, She sleeps, my la - dy sleeps! She sleeps! She sleeps, my la - dy sleeps!
sil - ver light, She sleeps, my la - dy sleeps! She sleeps! She sleeps, my la - dy sleeps!
slum-bers light, She sleeps, my la - dy sleeps! She sleeps! She sleeps, my la - dy sleeps!

Silent Night
(Stille Nacht)
(V. 24243)

158

JOSEPH MÖHR, 1818

FRANZ GRÜBER, 1818

1. Si - lent night! Ho - ly night! All is calm, all is bright.
2. Si - lent night! Ho - ly night! Shep - herds quake at the sight!
3. Si - lent night! Ho - ly night! Son of God, love's pure light!

'Round yon vir - gin moth - er and child! Ho - ly In - fant, so ten - der and mild,
Glo - ries stream from heav - en a - far, Heav'n-ly hosts sing, "Al - le - lu - ia!"
Ra - diant beams from Thy ho - ly face With the dawn of re - deem - ing grace,

Sleep in heav - en - ly peace, Sleep in heav - en - ly peace.
Christ, the Sav - ior, is born! Christ, the Sav - ior, is born!
Je - sus, Lord, at Thy birth, Je - sus, Lord, at Thy birth.

Old Folks at Home

(V. 21950)

S.C.F.

STEPHEN C. FOSTER

Con espressione

1. {'Way down up-on de Swa-nee Riv-er, Far, far a-way,
   {All up and down de whole cre-a-tion, Sad-ly I roam,
2. {All roun' de lit-tle farm I wan-dered, When I was young;
   {When I was play-ing with my broth-er, Hap-py was I;
3. {One lit-tle hut a-mong de bush-es, One that I love,
   {When will I see de bees a-hum-ming All roun' de comb?

Dere's wha my heart is turn-ing ev-er, Dere's wha de old folks stay.
Still long-ing for de old plan-ta-tion, And for de old folks at home.
Den man-y hap-py days I squan-der'd Man-y de songs I ___ sung.
Oh! take me to my kind old moth-er, Dere let me live and ___ die.
Still sad-ly to my mem-'ry rush-es, No mat-ter where I ___ rove.
When will I hear de ban-jo tum-ming, Down in my good old ___ home?

CHORUS

All de world am sad and drear-y, Ev-'ry-where I roam;

Oh, dark-ies, how my heart grows wear-y, Far from de old folks at home.

-138-

It Came upon the Midnight Clear

(V. 24243)

EDMUND H. SEARS, 1850

RICHARD S. WILLIS, 1851

Con Animato

1. It came up-on the mid-night clear, That glo-rious song of old, __
2. Still thro' the clo-ven skies they come, With peace-ful wings un-furled;
3. O ye be-neath life's crush-ing load, Whose forms are bend-ing low, __
4. For lo! the days are has-t'ning on, By proph-ets seen of old, __

From an-gels bend-ing near the earth, To touch their harps of gold: __
And still their heav'n-ly mu-sic floats O'er all the wea-ry world:
Who toil a-long the climb-ing way With pain-ful steps and slow; __
When with the ev-er-cir-cling years Shall come the time fore-told, __

"Peace on the earth, good will to men From heav'n's all gra-cious King,"
A-bove its sad and low-ly plains They bend on hov-'ring wing, __
Look now, for glad and gold-en hours Come swift-ly on the wing; __
When the new heav'n and earth shall own The Prince of Peace their King, __

The world in sol-emn still-ness lay To hear the an-gels sing. __
And ev-er o'er its Ba-bel sounds The bless-ed an-gels sing. __
Oh rest be-side the wea-ry road And hear the an-gels sing. __
And the whole world send back the song Which now the an-gels sing. __

161 O Come, All Ye Faithful

LATIN, 17th CENTURY

Translated by FREDERICK OAKELEY

(Adeste Fideles)

(V. 24243)

JOHN READING (?

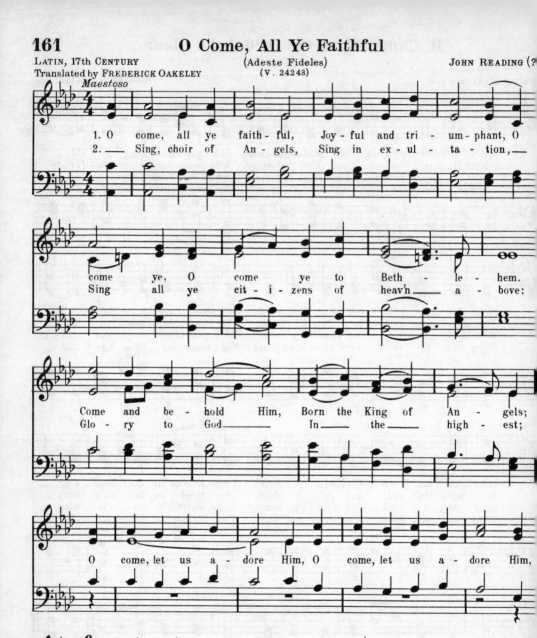

1. O come, all ye faithful, Joy- ful and tri - um- phant, O come ye, O come ye to Beth - le - hem. Come and be - hold Him, Born the King of An - gels; O come, let us a - dore Him, O come, let us a - dore Him, O come, let us a - dore Him, Christ, the Lord.

2. Sing, choir of An - gels, Sing in ex - ul - ta - tion, Sing all ye cit - i - zens of heav'n a - bove: Glo - ry to God In the high - est;

The First Noel

(V. 20993-CHIMES)

TRADITIONAL VERSION

TRADITIONAL
16TH CENTURY, FRENCH

mf Andantino

1. The first No - el the an - gels did say Was to
2. They look - ed up and saw a star Shin - ing
3. And by the light of that same star, Three
4. This star drew nigh to the north - west, O'er
5. Then en - ter'd in those Wise - men three, Full

cer - tain poor shep-herds in fields as they lay: In fields where they lay
in the east be - yond them far, And to the earth it
Wise - men came from coun - try far, To seek for a King was
Beth - le - hem it took its rest, And there it did both
rev - 'rent - ly up - on their knee, And of - fer'd there in

keep - ing their sheep On a cold win - ter's night that was so deep.
gave great light, And so it con - tinued both day and night.
their in - tent, And to fol - low the star wher - ev - er it went.
stop and stay Right o - ver the place where Je - sus lay.
His pres - ence, Their gold and myrrh and frank - in - cense.

f CHORUS

No - el, No - el, No - el, No - el, Born is the King of Is - ra - el.

Columbia, the Gem of the Ocean

(V. 22083)

THOMAS A'BECKET

Allegro

1. O Co - lum - bia, the gem of the o - cean, The __ home of the brave and the free, The __ shrine of each pa - triot's de - vo - tion, A __ world of - fers hom - age to thee. Thy man - dates make he - roes as - sem - ble, When Lib - er - ty's form stands in view; Thy

2. When war winged its wide des - o - la - tion, And __ threat-en'd the land to de - form, The __ ark then of free - dom's foun - da - tion, Co - lum - bia rode safe thro' the storm: With her gar - lands of vic - t'ry a - round her, When so proud - ly she bore her brave crew; With her

3. The __ star span - gled ban - ner bring hith - er, O'er Co - lum - bia's true sons let it wave; May the wreaths they have won nev - er with - er, Nor its stars cease to shine on the brave: May the serv - ice, u - nit - ed ne'er sev - er, But __ hold to their col - ors so true; The

ban-ners make tyr - an - ny trem-ble, / When borne by the red, white, and blue!
flag proud-ly float-ing be - fore her, / The boast of the red, white, and blue!
ar - my and na - vy for - ev - er, / Three cheers for the red, white, and blue!

When borne by the red, white, and blue! / When borne by the red, white, and blue!
The boast of the red, white, and blue! / The boast of the red, white, and blue!
Three cheers for the red, white, and blue! / Three cheers for the red, white, and blue!

Thy — ban-ners make tyr - an - ny trem-ble, / When borne by the red, white, and blue!
With her flag proud-ly float-ing be - fore her, / The boast of the red, white, and blue!
The — ar - my and na - vy for - ev - er, / Three cheers for the red, white, and blue!

Lovely Evening

147

(Round)

Allegretto

1.
Oh, how love - ly is the eve - ning, is the

2.
eve - ning, When the bells are sweet - ly ring - ing, sweet - ly

3.
ring - ing! Ding, dong, ding, dong, ding, dong.

The Star-Spangled Banner

(Service Version)

(V. 21428)

Francis Scott Key

John Stafford Smith

1. O___ say! can you see, by the dawn's ear-ly light, What so proud-ly we hail'd at the twi-light's last gleam-ing? Whose broad stripes and bright stars, thro' the per-il-ous fight, O'er the ram-parts we watch'd, were so gal-lant-ly stream-ing? And the rock-et's red glare, the bombs burst-ing in air, Gave proof thro' the night that our flag was still there. O___ say does that

2. On the shore, dim-ly seen thro' the mists of the deep, Where the foe's haughty host in dread si-lence re-pos-es, What is that which the breeze, o'er the tow-er-ing steep, As it fit-ful-ly blows, half con-ceals, half dis-clos-es? Now it catch-es the gleam of the morn-ing's first beam, In full glo-ry re-flect-ed now shines on the stream; 'Tis the Star-span-gled

3. O___ thus be it ev-er when free-men shall stand Be-tween their lov'd homes and the war's des-o-la-tion! Blest with vic-t'ry and peace, may the heav'n-res-cued land Praise the Pow'r that hath made and pre-served us a na-tion! Then con-quer we must, when our cause it is just, And this be our mot-to: "In God is our trust!" And the Star-span-gled

Chorus

broaden *ff*

Star-span-gled Ban-ner yet wave O'er the land of the free and the home of the brave?
Ban-ner, O long may it wave O'er the land of the free and the home of the brave!
Ban-ner in tri-umph shall wave O'er the land of the free and the home of the brave!

ff

America
(V. 21428)

175

SAMUEL FRANCIS SMITH

HENRY CAREY (?)

Maestoso *mf*

1. My coun-try, 'tis of thee, Sweet land of lib-er-ty,
2. My na-tive coun-try, thee, Land of the no-ble free,
3. Let mu-sic swell the breeze, And ring from all the trees,
4. Our fa-thers' God to Thee, Au-thor of lib-er-ty,
5. Our glo-rious land to-day, 'Neath ed-u-ca-tion's sway,
6. Thy safe-guard, lib-er-ty, The school shall ev-er be

Of thee I sing. Land where my fa-thers died! Land of the
Thy name I love. I love thy rocks and rills, Thy woods and
Sweet free-dom's song. Let mor-tal tongues a-wake; Let all that
To Thee we sing. Long may our land be bright With free-dom's
Soars up-ward still. Its halls of learn-ing fair, Whose boun-ties
Our na-tion's pride! No ty-rant hand shall smite, While with en-

ff

Pil-grim's pride! From ev-'ry moun-tain-side, Let free-dom ring!
tem-pled hills; My heart with rap-ture thrills Like that a-bove.
breathe par-take; Let rocks their si-lence break, The sound pro-long.
ho-ly light; Pro-tect us by Thy might, Great God, our King!
all may share, Be-hold them ev-'ry-where, On vale and hill!
cir-cling might All there are taught the Right With Truth al-lied.

176 America, the Beautiful
(V 22083)

KATHARINE LEE BATES

SAMUEL A. WARD

Grandioso

1. O beau-ti-ful for spa-cious skies, For am-ber waves of grain,— For
2. O beau-ti-ful for pil-grim feet Whose stern im-pas-sion'd stress— A
3. O beau-ti-ful for he-roes prov'd In lib-er-at-ing strife,— Who
4. O beau-ti-ful for pa-triot dream That sees be-yond the years— Thine

pur-ple moun-tain maj-es-ties A-bove the fruit-ed plain.— A-
thor-ough-fare for free-dom beat A-cross the wil-der-ness.— A-
more than self their coun-try loved, And mer-cy more than life.— A-
al-a-bas-ter cit-ies gleam Un-dimmed by hu-man tears.— A-

mer-i-ca! A-mer-i-ca! God shed His grace on thee,— And
mer-i-ca! A-mer-i-ca! God mend thine ev-'ry flaw,— Con-
mer-i-ca! A-mer-i-ca! May God thy gold re-fine— Till
mer-i-ca! A-mer-i-ca! God shed His grace on thee,— And

crown thy good with bro-ther-hood From sea to shin-ing sea.
firm thy soul in self-con-trol, Thy lib-er-ty in law.
all suc-cess be no-ble-ness, And ev-'ry gain di-vine.
crown thy good with bro-ther-hood From sea to shin-ing sea.

Lullaby

FRANK AMES POWER
Arr. C.L.P.

Slum-ber my ba-by, no harm need you fear. Hush-a-bye, rock-a-bye ba-by

Noth-ing can harm you while moth-er is near. Hush-a-bye, rock-a-bye,

bye_____ You have been play-ing so hard all day long,

Sleep-y eyes close with the lul-la-by song. Moth-er will keep you from

harm and from wrong, Hush-a-bye, rock-a-bye, ba - by.

CHORUS

Hush - a - bye, rock - a - bye, lul - la - by low,

Hush - a - bye, rock - a - bye, ba - by. Moth-er will keep you from

harm and from wrong, Hush - a - bye, rock - a - bye, bye.____

Good Morning, Merry Sunshine

Brightly

1. Good morn-ing, mer-ry sun-shine, How did you wake so
2. I nev-er go to sleep, dear child, I just go 'round to

soon? You scared the lit-tle stars a-way, And shined a-way the
see My lit-tle chil-dren of the east, Who rise and watch for

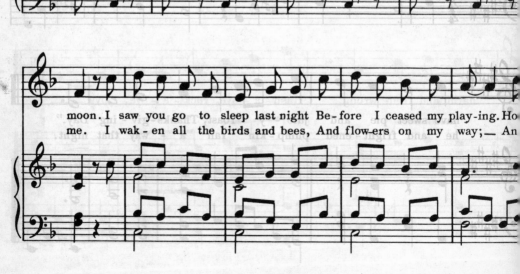

moon. I saw you go to sleep last night Be-fore I ceased my play-ing. Ho
me. I wak-en all the birds and bees, And flow-ers on my way;— An

Good Morning, Merry Sunshine

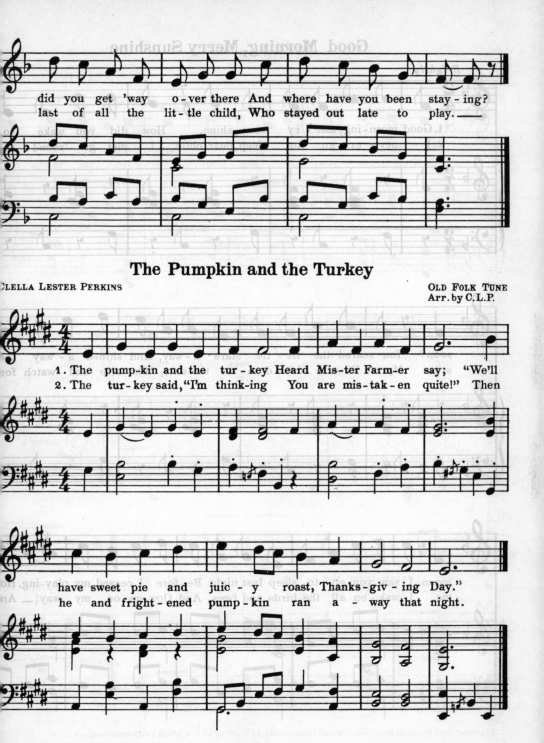

did you get 'way   o - ver there And where have you been stay - ing?
last of all the   lit - tle child, Who stayed out late to   play.___

The Pumpkin and the Turkey

CLELLA LESTER PERKINS

OLD FOLK TUNE
Arr. by C.L.P.

1. The pump-kin and the tur - key Heard Mis-ter Farm-er say; "We'll
2. The tur-key said, "I'm think-ing You are mis-tak-en quite!" Then

have sweet pie and   juic - y   roast, Thanks-giv - ing Day."
he   and fright - ened pump - kin ran   a - way that night.

Rainbow Song

UNKNOWN

Air from OFFENBA

Soft - ly falls the A - pril rain, The clouds are sail - ing
Love - ly rain - bow, hang - ing there, A - bove the tall - est

high. Gen - tle breez - es push them back, Like
tree, Like a fair - y bridge you seem, Be -

Fine.

cur - tains from the sky.
tween the sky and me. Now the gold - en

cresc.

Reprinted from the April 1915 issue of Normal Instructor, by courtesy of F. A. Owen Publishing Company.

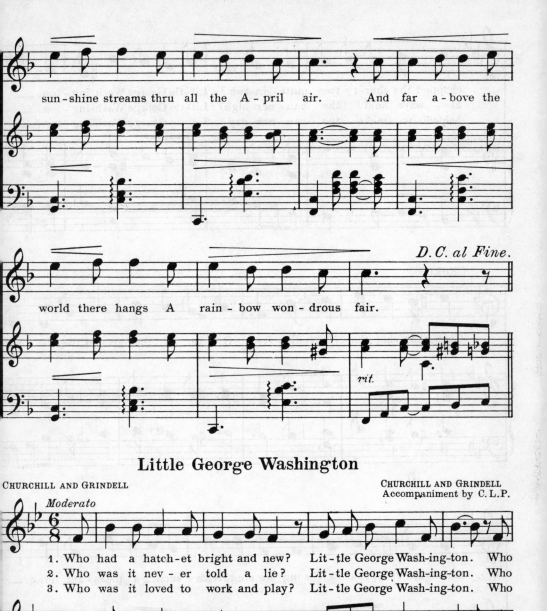

sun-shine streams thru all the A-pril air. And far a-bove the

world there hangs A rain-bow won-drous fair.

D.C. al Fine.

rit.

Little George Washington

CHURCHILL AND GRINDELL

CHURCHILL AND GRINDELL
Accompaniment by C.L.P.

Moderato

mp

1. Who had a hatch-et bright and new? Lit-tle George Wash-ing-ton. Who
2. Who was it nev-er told a lie? Lit-tle George Wash-ing-ton. Who
3. Who was it loved to work and play? Lit-tle George Wash-ing-ton. Who

chopped the cher-ry tree quite in two? Lit-tle George Wash-ing-ton.
al - ways held the ban-ner high? Lit-tle George Wash-ing-ton.
helped to make the ban-ner gay? Lit-tle George Wash-ing-ton.

CHORUS

Chop, chop, chop, the bright chips fly, O - ver all the ground they lie And

hatch-ets ring, as a song we sing With such a pleas-ant ring.

The Big, Bad Mouse

F. A. P.

FRANK AMES POWER
Accompaniment by G. C.

BOYS

1. There was a lit - tle mouse as the
2. O now a cat is brav - er than a

sto - ries say— He was mod - est as a mouse should
girl, it seems, For the cat, he did - n't run a -

be;   Till he met a bunch of girls   in the
way,   So the mous-ie gave a yell   and he

house   one   day,   And they gave   an aw-ful shriek   and
swelled his   chest,   And   dou-bled up his fist   and

GIRLS   BOYS

ran   a - way, And he said; (What did   he   say?) And he
did   his best, And he said; (What did   he   say?) And he

said; (What did he say?) And the mous - ie said, said he:
said; (What did he say?) And these last few words said he:

CHORUS

What a big bad mouse am I! I could win the whole world if I

tried. When I raise my voice how the girls do run; I'll

hunt up the cat and I'll have some fun. So he swelled his chest till he

near - ly split his vest, this big bad ter - ri - ble mouse.

Pop Corn Song

UNKNOWN

UNKNOWN
Accompaniment by C. L. P

Lightly

1. We
2. We

love   to   sit be - side the fire, Up - on a win - ter's
chat and laugh and sing a song, So hap - py ev' - ry

night, And watch the pop - ping of the corn, so mer - ry and so
one, And stand a - round the cheer-ful fire, to wait 'till the corn is

Fine. CHORUS *Allegro*
                  staccato

light. Then pop, pop, pop, pop, pop. Then pop, pop, pop, pop, pop. Then
done.

pop, pop, pop, pop, pop, pop, pop, pop, pop. Then

pop, pop, pop, pop, pop. Then pop, pop, pop, pop, pop. Then

pop, pop, pop, pop, pop, pop, pop, pop, pop.

D.S

D.S

Santa's Cake

UNKNOWN

CLELLA LESTER PERKINS

Brightly

1. I saved my cake for San - ta Claus, One Christ-mas eve, at
2. When ev' - ry one was fast a - sleep Ev' - ry one but

tea. For if rid - ing makes one hun - gry, How
me, I tip - toed in - to ma - ma's room, O

hun - gry he must be; I put it on the
just as still, to see If he had been there

chim - ney shelf Where he'd be sure to go. I
yet; Dear me! It made my feel - ings ache, There

poco rit.   *a tempo*

think it does a per - son good, To be re - mem - bered so.
sat a mis-er-'ble, lit - tle mouse ___ Eat-ing San - ta's cake.

poco rit.

a tempo

A Sailor Dear

Hazel Louise Brown   Clella Lester Perkins

With tenderness
p

1. Ba - by's a sail - or dear, Swing, ba - by swing:
2. Sail on the slum - ber sea, Swing, ba - by swing:

legato

p

Sail - ing far and sail - ing near, Swing, ba - by swing.—
Ti - ny boat will car - ry thee, Swing, ba - by swing.—

CHORUS

Swing ba - by, swing ba - by, Swing ba - by swing,—

Swing ba - by, swing ba - by, Swing ba - by swing.—

2nd time repeat chorus, humming very softly.

The Goblin Man

SALLIE G. FITZGERALD

1. The Gob-lin Man he comes a-round, look out! look out! He'll car-ry you off to Gob-lin town, look out! look out! And if you're good he will not stay, But

2. The Gob-lin Man he creeps up slow, look out! look out! He al-ways knows which way to go, look out! look out! You nev-er know when he's a-round, The

Reprinted from the October 1922 issue of Normal Instructor and Primary Plans by courtesy of F. A. Owen Publishing Co.

turn a - round and run a - way, But oh, my child, if
naugh - ty boy — he's al - ways found, So now I've warned you,

rit.

you are bad, look out! look out!
chil - dren dear, look out! look out!

a tempo

Betsy Ross

UNKNOWN

GERMAN STUDENTS' SONG
Arr. by C.L.P.

mf

1. Who made the first flag? Bet - sy Ross, Bet - sy Ross. She
2. The stars had five points for she looked up - on high; And
3. And on the blue field she left plen - ty of room, A

made it of cot - ton and wool - en and floss. Who__
saw how they glim - mered a - far in the sky. And for
star for each state how e'er man - y might come. And__

taught her the way? 'Twas the first pres - i - dent; He
each of the thir - teen states to be - gin, A
this flag is wav - ing for me and for you; It's

planned and she sewed for she knew what he meant.
red stripe, a white stripe, she count - ed them in.
wav - ing to - day with its red, white and blue.

I Hear a Little Tapping

F.A.P.

FRANK AMES POWER
Accompaniment by C.L.P.

1. I hear a lit-tle tap-ping on my win-dow pane, Can an-y bod-y guess what it is? There's a rob-in hop hop-ping, but I

2. I hear a lit-tle step-ping out a-cross the lawn, Can an-y bod-y guess what it is? There's a bob-o-link sing-ing, but I'm

3. I heard a pop, pop, pop-ping in the ap-ple tree, Can an-y bod-y guess what it is? There's a lit-tle bird knit-ting a new

don't think it's he, Or the wood - peck - er chop-ping on the
sure it isn't he, Nor the blue - bells,— ring — 'neath the
nest up — there, And a hum-ming bird — flit - ting thro' the

hol - low tree. I hear a lit - tle tap-ping on my
ma - ple tree. I hear a lit - tle tap-ping out a -
sum - mer air. I hear a pop, pop, pop-ping in the

poco rit.   CHORUS

win - dow pane, Can an - y - bod - y guess what it is? It's ___
cross the lawn, Can an - y - bod - y guess what it is? It's the
ap - ple tree, Can an - y - bod - y guess what it is? It's the

poco rit.

a tempo

rain-drops fall - ing, — fall - ing from the sky. Winds are call - ing,
spring come, com - ing, — step-ping on the lawn, Bees are hum - ming,
buds pop, pop, pop-ping out to meet the spring, Toad hop, hop, hop-ping,

a tempo

call - ing with a sigh, But the tip - py, tip - py tap And —
win - ter time is gone, But the step - py, — step, And the
wish-ing he could sing, But the pop, pop, pop, pop, pop, And the

ritard - - - -

tip - py, tip - py tap Keeps call - ing, and call - ing for me.
step-py, step-py step Keeps call - ing, and call - ing for me.
hop, hop, hop, hop, hop, Keeps call - ing, and call - ing for me.

ritard

Marching Song

F. A. P.

FRANK AMES POWER
Accompaniment by C. L.

See the sol-diers march-ing down the street. Hip hur - ray! Hip hur

ray! Hip hur - ray! Heads up straight with u - ni-forms so neat. Hip hur

ray! Hip hur - ray! Hur - ray! They look so fine as they

march a - long the line, They're as brave and bold As the

fear - less knights of old. Hear the tramp - ing of the feet, To the

drum-mer's mer-ry beat. Hip hur-ray! Hip hur-ray! Hur - ray.

On Easter Eve

ELEANOR JEWETT

CLELLA LESTER PERKINS

Allegretto

1. Lit - tle East - er Bun - ny Found that he was late;
2. Rolled right down the rain - bow, Got in - to the dye.

legato

Had to hur - ry, hur - ry, So chil - dren should not wait.
Bun - ny had to chase them All a - cross the sky.

mf

Stum - bled on the rain - bow Let his bas - ket fall.
East - er Bun - ny picked them up, Col - ored red and green. "Thes

Courtesy of the author and the Chicago Tribune.

Good - ness me! his East - er eggs Tum - bled, one and all!
are", he laughed; "the fin - est eggs That I have ev - er seen!"

After 2nd Stanza

East - er Bun - ny hur - ried, Hid them as he went,

p *ritard* - - - - - *mf a tempo*

But he nev - er, nev - er told A - bout his ac - ci - dent.

ritard

a tempo

Boy Scout March

M.S.M.

MARY SANFORD MORRIS

mf *In march time, with spirit.*

1. Shoul - der to shoul - der, firm and stead - y,
2. When comes the sun - ny sum - mer weath - er,
3. Scouts nev - er fail a weak - er broth - er:

Eyes straight a - head and heads held high, Ban - ners a - float and
Off to the woods and streams they go, Learn - ing, in long, glad
Wound - ed or sick, they help him thro', And ev - er stand by

knap - sacks read - y, That's how the Scout Pa -
days to - geth - er, All that a good Boy
one an - oth - er, As loy - al Scouts are

Boy Scout March

trol   goes   by!   They   are   the   lads   who   know   the   way
Scout   should   know,   Woods-men   and   camp-ers   they   must   be
pledged   to   do,   Dai - ly   they   do   some   kind - ly   deed;

To   make   the   most   of   ev - 'ry   day;   Nev - er   a   care   nor   a
Friends   of   each   bird   and   flow'r   and   tree;   Na - ture's   their   com - rade,   by
Ev - er   they   an - swer   calls   of   need;   Serv - ice   is   part   of   their

cresc.

fear   have   they!___   Hark   to   their   march - ing   song:
land   or   sea,___   Mak - ing   them   brave   and   strong.
knight-ly   creed,___   Help - ing   the   world   a - long.

- 175 -

Here's to the Scout, where-e'er you find him,
Stead-fast of heart and strong of hand! Here's to the law and
oath that bind him True to God and na-tive land!

PART FOUR

Fundamentals of Music

In addition to all of the fundamental musical information needed by the classroom teacher in the elementary school, the following section contains much that will be found useful and informative in a further study of the subject.

GLOSSARY OF MUSICAL TERMS

a cappella (ä käp-pĕl'lä). Without instrumental accompaniment.

accel., accelerando (ät-chă-lĕ-rän'dō). Increase the speed.

adagio (á-dä'jō). Slowly. Leisurely.

ad libitum (ăd lĭb'ĭ-tŭm). Tempo and expression may be decided by the performer.

al
alla } to the; in the style of.

allegretto (äl'lā-grĕt'tō). Lively.

allegro (äl-lā'grō). Quick. Cheerful. Brisk.

andante (än-dän'tā). Slow. A walking tempo.

andantino (än'dän-tē'nō). Slow.

animato (ä'nē-mä'tō). Spirited. With animation.

ardente (är-dĕn'tē). Ardently.

assai (äs-sä-ē). Very.

a tempo (ä tĕm'pō). In time. Used after any change in the movement of a piece to direct a return to the original rate of speed.

bolero (bŏ-lā'rō). A lively Spanish dance.

brio (brē'ō). Vigor. Fire.

calando (kä-län'dō). Diminishing and retarding.

cantabile (kän-tä'bĕ-lä). Flowing. In a singing style.

col. With the.

con (kŏn). With.

cresc., crescendo (krĕ-shĕn'dō). Gradually louder.

D.C., da capo (dä kä'pō). A sign of repetition. "From the beginning."

decresc., decrescendo (dā-krĕsh-ĕn'-dō). Diminishing in loudness.

di (dē). Of, with, for, from, by, etc.

dim., diminuendo (dĭ-mĭn'ū-ĕn'dō). Gradually softer.

dolce (dōl'chä). Sweet. Soft.

D.S., dal segno (däl sā'nyō). A sign of repetition, indicating that a part of the composition is to be repeated beginning at the sign and ending with *"Fine"*

e (ā). And

espressione (ĕs-prĕs-sĭ-ō'nĕ). With feeling.

f., forte (fôr'tā). Loud. Strong.

ff., fortissimo (fôr-tĭs'ĭ-mō). Very loud.

fine (fē'nā). The end.

fz., forzando (för-tsän'-dō). Forced; sharply emphasized.

fuoco (fū-ó-kō). Fire; energy.

giocoso (jō-kō'sō). Humorously. Playfully.

giojoso (jō-yō'sō). Joyously.

grandioso (grän'dĕ-ō'sō). Grand. Noble.

grave (grä'vĕ). Very.

grazia (gräts'yä). Grace and elegance.

larghetto (lär-gĕt'tō). Rather slow.

largo (lär'gō). Very slow. Broad.

legato (lā-gä'tō). Smoothly; the tones closely linked together.

leggiero (lĕd-jā'rō). Light. Easy. Nimble.

lento (lĕn'tō). Slowly.

l'istesso tempo (lēs-tĕs'sō). The same tempo.

ma (mä). But. (Used in phrases.)

maestoso (mä'ĕs-tō'sō). Majestic. Dignified.

meno (mā'nō). Less.

meno mosso (mā'nō môs'sō). Not so fast.

mf., mezzo forte (mĕd'zō fôr'tä). Moderately loud.

moderato (mŏd'ĕ-rä'tō). In moderate tempo.

molto (mōl'tō). Much.

morendo (môr-ĕn'dō). Dying away. Diminishing.

moto (mō'tō). Motion.

mp., mezzo piano (mĕd'zō pĕ-ä'nō). Moderately soft.

non. Not.

p., piano (pĕ-ä'nō). Soft.

piu (pē-oo'). More.

piu mosso (pē-oo' môs'sō). More speed.

poco (pō'kō). A little. Somewhat.

poco a poco (pō'kō ä pō'kō). Little by little.

pp., pianissimo (pĕ'ä-nĭs'ĭ-mo). Very soft.

presto (prĕs'tō). Very fast.

quasi (kwä'zē). In the manner of, like, almost.

rall., rallentando (räl'lĕn-tän'dō). Gradually slower.

rf. or rfz., rinforzando (rĭn-fôr-tzän'dō). Sudden force and emphasis.

religioso (rä'lĕ-jō'sō). Solemnly. Devoutly.

rit., ritard., ritardando (rē'tär-dän'dō). Gradually becoming slower.

sempre (sĕm'prä). Always. Throughout.

sf., sforzando (sfôr-tsän'dō). Strong accent. Special emphasis.

smorz., smorzando (smôr-tzän'-dō). Dying away.

spirito (spē'rĭ-tō). With spirit. Lively.

stringendo (strĭn-jĕn'-dō). Hurrying.

sostenuto (sōs'tĕ-noo'tō). Sustained.

tempo (tĕm'pō). Time, rate of movement.

tranquillo (trän-kwēl'lō). Calm. Quiet.

valse (váls). A waltz.

vivace (vē-vä'chä). Lively. Quick.

FUNDAMENTALS OF MUSIC

Introduction

Music is the esthetic and emotional aspect of sound. Sound is very accurately defined as "something heard" but this definition is too general in meaning and application to give precise information as to the nature of music. The two great subdivisions of sound, tone and noise, are both products of a single universal principle, the law of wave-motion or vibra- tion. Tone results from the regular vibration of a sonorous body which is of such a nature as to produce a harmonious sound of definite pitch.* Noise results from irregular vibrations, is not harmonious, and has no definite pitch.

Tones may be produced by plucking or bowing as with stringed instru- ments such as the harp or the violin; by percussion as with gongs, bells, metal tubes, drums, and the piano; by vibrating membranes or reeds, as with the human voice, the clarinet, and the bassoon; or by means of a vibrating column of air as with organ pipes and the flute. With brass instruments the player's lips act as a membrane.

There are four characteristics of tone: length, pitch, intensity (power), and quality. Tone length refers to the duration of the sound—the actual time it is heard. Pitch is determined by the *number* of vibrations per second which produce the sound and give it its relative highness or lowness in the tonal series. Intensity, the degree of loudness, depends upon the *amplitude* of the vibrations. Quality (timbre) is determined by the *character* of the vibrations dependent on the nature of the instrument and the manner of producing the tone.

---

*The nature of vibration and its relation to pitch is well illustrated by the oscillations of a pen- dulum. The longer the rod or string the slower it will swing if allowed free motion. The lowest tone on the piano (A) is produced by the vibrations of a long string at the rate of 27 vibrations per second while the highest tone (C) has a very short string whose rate of vibration is 4224 per second. If a string two feet long under tension produces a certain pitch, one-half of its length under the same tension will produce the perfect octave above; and twice its length the perfect octave below. Expressed in terms of speed of vibration a sonorous body producing a tone of 64 vibrations per second must vibrate 128 times per second for the perfect octave above and 32 times per second to produce the perfect octave below that pitch. Therefore the vibrational ratio existing between a tone and its octave is 1 to 2.

A composer uses tone to express feelings, sentiments, ideas, as a painter uses colors and a writer words. A painter must organize his picture—arrange its objects and choose his colors—according to esthetic principles and the laws of form. Likewise the writer must have ideas, a vocabulary, and understand the laws of grammar and construction. The tone material used by the composer consists of but twelve different sounds and duplications of them at lower or higher pitches over a scope of seven octaves, comprising a total of about eighty-four tones.

In writing music a composer organizes tones in rhythmic relations according to certain laws governing the succession and combination of tones. The study of these laws is comprised under the general heading of the Theory of Music and with such branches as Rudiments, Harmony, Composition, Counterpoint, History, Esthetics, and Acoustics.

Ear Training. In listening to music one is aware of three distinct elements: melody, the horizontal aspect of music; harmony, the vertical aspect of music; and rhythm, the symmetrical grouping of the sounds.

Melody consists of a succession of single tones standing out clearly from the mass of sound and occupying a position of leadership in expressing the central musical idea. Harmony consists of the motion of massed tones which follow and support each curve of the melodic line and add to it color, depth, and emphasis. Both the melodic and harmonic aspects are united in a common rhythmic scheme which determines the character of the sound motion and groups the impressions into definite portions of time. All of these elements are perceived in relation to a specific tonal background that has for its center of gravity a single tone which is felt to be the foundation tone. If one is to listen to music intelligently the apprehension of each of these factors is essential. Pitch discrimination is the basic necessity and must be approached from a clear sense of tones in key relation.

Parallel with drill in pitch discrimination should come practice in sensing the duration and grouping of sounds (rhythm) and in the perception of intensity and quality. These characteristics of sound may be studied very profitably while listening to a performance in a concert hall or by radio.

Following practice in sensing of pitch relations between single tones should come drill in the recognition of intervals and qualities when two tones are sounded together. This brings to the student two effects in music which are of a fundamental nature—consonance and dissonance.

When tones are brought into combination the blending of the elements inherent in the separate tones gives rise to a new quality which is the sum of their individual qualities. Thus a triad, a three-toned chord, is much richer and more powerful in effect than any two of its tones.

It should be remembered that once the habit of exercising these discriminatory powers has been well grounded, ability will continue to increase without the need of extensive special drill. Particular attention should be paid to the quality of the sounds heard, not alone from the standpoint of differentiating between the tonal qualities of instruments, but also to the subtle changes from pitch to pitch and tone to tone of a single instrument. The symphony orchestra offers a bewildering variety of qualities in the playing of a simple chord while even the piano with its apparently limited resources as regards changes of quality can, when played by a real artist, afford a great diversity. The appreciation of beauty of tone in the abstract without regard to meaning or expression is an important factor in the enjoyment of music.

Notation

The basic knowledge necessary in the study of music—the signs and symbols used in its notation, the scales and chords upon which our music is founded, and much additional information—may be learned in the section which follows. The comprehension of this material ought to precede any practical work in the teaching or study of music.

Staff. The staff (or stave) consists of five horizontal lines and the spaces between them upon which music is written or printed.

Leger Lines. Leger lines are short lines placed above or below the staff to increase its extent. On these lines and the spaces they form are indicated pitches too high or too low to be represented on the staff.

Clef. A clef is a character placed upon the staff at the beginning of a piece of music which fixes the names and positions of the notes. There are two clefs in common use: the Treble or G clef which fixes the tone G on the second line of the staff, counting from the bottom; the Bass or F clef which fixes the tone F on the fourth line of the staff, counting from the bottom. There must be a clef for each staff.

Degree. The lines and spaces of the staff are called degrees: the first line (counting upward) being the first degree of the staff; the space just above, the second degree of the staff; the second line, the third degree; and so on. Likewise the space below the first line is the first degree below the staff, the first leger line below is the second degree below the staff, and so on. Leger lines and spaces above the staff are numbered similarly as first degree above the staff, second degree above the staff, and so on.

Middle C.   Middle C on the piano is the white key to the left of the group of two black keys nearest the middle of the keyboard just opposite the name of the instrument. In written or printed music middle C is indicated by a note placed upon the first leger line below the treble staff which is the same as the first line above the bass staff.

Interval.   An interval is the difference in pitch between two tones. In occidental music the smallest interval used is a half-step. Between any tone and its octave or eighth there are twelve half-steps at equal intervals, approximately, one from the other.

Half-step.   A half-step is the smallest interval between two tones. On the piano, a half-step is the distance from any key to the one nearest it to the right or left, whether white key or black key. For example, the following are half-steps: E to F, F to F♯; F♯ to G, and so on.

Whole-step.   A whole-step consists of two half-steps. For example, the following are whole-steps: C to D, G to A, D to E, and so on.

Sharp and Double-Sharp.   A sharp is a character which, when placed before a note on the staff, raises it in pitch one half-step. A double-sharp raises it one whole-step.

Flat and Double-flat.   A flat is a character which, when placed before a note on the staff, lowers it in pitch one half-step. A double-flat lowers it one whole-step.

Natural.   A natural cancels the effect of a previous sharp or flat.

Accidentals (Chromatic Signs).   The sharps, flats, and naturals which do not belong to the key, yet are used in the notation of a piece of music, are called accidentals or chromatic signs.

Tone Names.   Seven letters A, B, C, D, E, F, and G are used to name the tones.

Measure.   The grouping of tones from one principal accent to another is called a measure.

Bars. Vertical lines placed upon the staff and used to separate the measures are called bars.

The Piano Keyboard and the Letter Names of the Degrees of the Staves

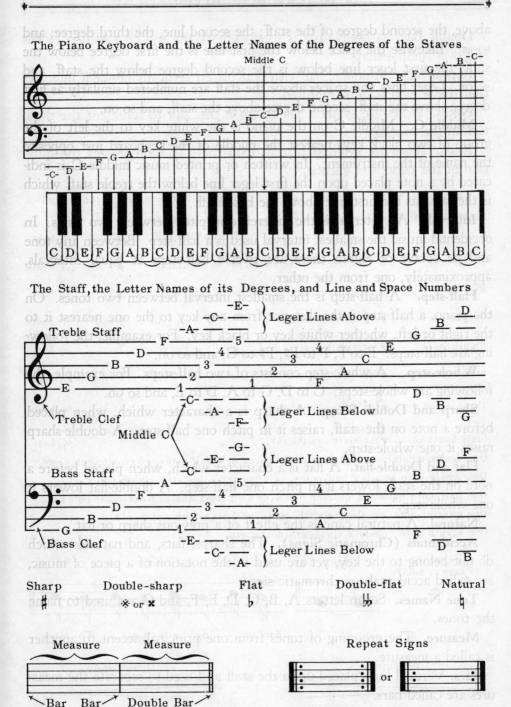

Middle C

The Staff, the Letter Names of its Degrees, and Line and Space Numbers

Leger Lines Above
Treble Staff

Treble Clef
Leger Lines Below
Middle C

Leger Lines Above
Bass Staff

Bass Clef
Leger Lines Below

Sharp   Double-sharp   Flat   Double-flat   Natural

Measure   Measure   Repeat Signs

Bar   Bar   Double Bar   or

Double Bar. A double bar is used to mark the end of a section or the end of a composition.

Repeat Sign. A double bar with dots placed vertically beside it indicates that the section is to be repeated.

Notes. Notes are symbols placed upon the staff to represent the duration of the sounds.

Rests. Rests are symbols placed upon the staff to represent the duration of the periods of silence.

The most common notes and rests and their relative duration are given below:

Double-whole-note ‖O‖ or double - whole-rest (between 3rd and 4th

lines of the staff) . . . . . . 8 beats

Whole-note. . . . O or whole-rest (below 4th line of the staff) . . . . 4 beats

Half-note . . . . ♩ or half-rest (above 3rd line of the staff) . . . . . . 2 beat

Quarter- note. . . ♩ or quarter-rest. . . . . ⅄ or ⌇ . . 1 beat

Eighth - note . . . ♪ or eighth-rest . . . . ⅄ . . . . ½ beat

Sixteenth - note. . ♬ or sixteenth-rest. . . . . ⅄ . . . . ¼ beat

Thirty-second-note . ♬ or thirty-second-rest . . . . ⅄ . . . . ⅛ beat

Sixty-fourth-note . ♬ or sixty-fourth-rest. . . . . ⅄ . . . . ¹⁄₁₆ beat

One double-whole-note equals 2 whole-notes, or 4 half-notes, or 8 quarter-notes, etc.

One whole-note equals 2 half-notes, or 4 quarter-notes, or 8 eighth-notes, etc.

One half-note equals 2 quarter-notes, or 4 eighth-notes, or 8 sixteenth-notes, etc.

One quarter-note equals 2 eighth-notes, or 4 sixteenth-notes, etc.

One eighth-note equals 2 sixteenth-notes, etc.

Dot. A dot placed to the right of a note or rest adds to its duration one-half. Two dots add three-quarters to its duration. For example, a whole-note with a dot equals three half-notes, six quarter-notes, or twelve eighth-notes, et cetera. A half-note with a dot equals three quarter-notes, six eighth-notes, or twelve sixteenth-notes, et cetera. A half-note with two dots equals three quarter-notes and one eighth-note, seven eighth-notes, or fourteen sixteenth-notes, et cetera. The same applies to rests.

Fermata (Pause or Hold). A fermata is a sign used to indicate that the note or rest over or under which it is placed should be prolonged beyond its normal duration.

Staccato. A dot placed over a note indicates that the note should be performed in a short disconnected manner.

Accent. A short horizontal line placed over a note indicates that the note should receive an agogic accent—an emphasis perceptible as a slight prolongation of the tone but not of force or stress.

A V-shaped sign placed either horizontally or vertically over a note indicates that the note is to be performed with extra force.

Tie. A short curved line closely connecting the heads of two notes adjoining each other on the same degree of the staff is called a tie. It indicates that only one tone is to be sounded equal to the combined duration of the two notes.

Slur. The slur is a curved line used to join notes together and has a significance depending upon the particular context. Some of its uses are: *in vocal music,* to indicate that the two or more notes thus connected are to be sung on a single word or syllable; to indicate sustained or connected tones (legato); *in instrumental music,* when a slur is used to join two notes of different pitch they should be closely joined, the first note receiving a slight agogic accent; *to group irregular note values* within the measure, in which case a figure is added indicating the number of notes in the group (see triplet and doublet); *as a phrase line* to show that all the notes included within it belong together in the expression of a musical idea.

Crescendo and Decrescendo or Diminuendo. A crescendo is a gradual increase in intensity of tone. A decrescendo or diminuendo is a gradual decrease in the intensity of tone.

Stems of Notes. Whether the stems of notes are turned upward on the right side of the head or downward on the left side depends upon their position on the staff. If a note is below the third line the stem should be placed on the right side and turned upward. If the note is on or above the third line the stem should be placed on the left side and turned downward. The foregoing is the rule except that when two or more voice parts are written on a single staff the stems of the notes of the upper part are turned upwards and those of the lower part downward.

Ottava alta (8ᵛᵃ). To be played or sung one octave higher.

The Scales*

A scale in music is a succession of tones based upon a given fundamental and proceeding in consecutive order to its octave or eighth.

The scales most used by composers are the diatonic and chromatic. The word *diatonic* means "through the tones." Major and minor scales are called diatonic because they contain both whole-steps and half-steps and move from line to space and space to line throughout the degrees of the staff with only one tone on each degree. The chromatic scale is composed exclusively of half-steps.

---

*If a sonorous body be set in vibration to sound any given pitch, in addition to the primary sound a number of other sounds are produced in an ascending series each one of which is of less intensity than the preceding. These affiliated tones are called overtones or upper partial tones. The reason for this effect is that a vibrating body not only vibrates over its whole length but also in smaller segments or loops. The points of division are called nodes. The vibration of the whole string, for example, produces the primary tone; a division into two equal parts, the first overtone, one octave higher in pitch; a division into three equal parts the next overtone, the interval of a twelfth above the primary tone; a division into four equal parts the next overtone, the interval of two octaves above the primary tone, et cetera. Tone is thus compound in nature. The richer the tone, the greater the number of overtones.

Starting from the tone C as a fundamental, the upper partial tones occur in the following order: C, C¹ (the octave above), G¹, C² (the second octave), E², G², A², B² (approximately), C³ (the third octave), D³, E³. The first tone with a different letter name from the fundamental tone to appear in this series of overtones is G, the fifth above C (if brought into close proximity). G is thus the nearest related *different* tone to C. G, if used as a fundamental, will have D, the fifth above, as its nearest related *different* tone. Proceeding in this manner by what is called the circle of fifths, the following ascending series is obtained: C-D-A-E-B-F♯. C, the fundamental, is already the fifth above F, therefore it is preferred in the series instead of F♯. Drawn closely together and placed in order these tones form the scale of C major, C-D-E-F-G-A-B-C. These tones are not only closely related to the fundamental tone but also to each other.

The great point of difference between the major and minor scales lies in the pitch of the third tone which is one half-step lower in the minor than in the major scale. This gives the minor scale a rather somber plaintive character compared with the bright cheerful major scale.

The tones of the scale are numbered and are called degrees of the scale. Thus the first tone of a scale is called the first degree (1); the second, the second degree (2); the third, the third degree (3), etc. The Syllable names are:

do, re, mi, fa, sol, la, ti, do*
1   2   3   4   5   6   7   8

The specific names of the tones of the scale are: (1) Tonic, (2) Super-Tonic, (3) Mediant, (4) Sub-Dominant, (5) Dominant, (6) Sub-Mediant, (7) Leading-tone, (8) Octave.

Key. The close relationship existing between the tones derived from a given fundamental tone is called a key. Hence in speaking of the Key of C reference is made not only to the scale but also to all the chords belonging to it.

Scale and Key Names. Any pitch may serve as the tonic or key-tone of a scale, and the scale and key takes its name from the letter name of this tone.

Tetrachord. The first or second group of four tones of an octave in any diatonic scale is called a tetrachord.

Major Scale. The major scale is a succession of eight tones separated by whole-steps except between 3 and 4, and 7 and 8, where half-steps occur. This pattern is invariable for all major scales.

C Major Scale. Starting with the tone middle C the following major scale may be formed:

1 — 2 — 3 ⌣ 4 — 5 — 6 — 7 ⌣ 8
C — D — E ⌣ F — G — A — B ⌣ C†
⌊ Tetrachord ⌋   ⌊ Tetrachord ⌋

The scale consists of two tetrachords of identical construction, and each of these tetrachords (C—D—E–F and G—A—B–C) has the following succession of intervals: whole-step, whole-step, half-step. There is a whole-step between the tetrachords.

---

*In pronouncing the syllable names of the tones of the scale sound e like a in day; i like e in we; and a like a in father.

†Starting at this point, in all diagrams and illustrations which follow a straight line between letter names, scale degree numbers, or notes indicates a whole-step; a curved line indicates a half-step.

C Major Scale

C __ D __ E ⌣ F __ G __ A __ B ⌣ C
do __ re __ mi ⌣ fa __ sol __ la __ ti ⌣ do

The Scales and Keys having Sharps. Using the upper tetrachord of the Key of C (G—A—B⌣C) to form the first half of a new scale and adding another tetrachord above, we obtain the following succession: G—A—B⌣C D—E⌣F—G. Since the two tetrachords must be of identical construction it will be found necessary to place a sharp before the seventh note (F) in order to have the necessary whole-step between E and F (6 and 7) and a half-step between F and G (7 and 8). Thus a new scale, the G Major Scale, is obtained. Other scales having sharps are formed in a like manner.

Formation of the G Major Scale

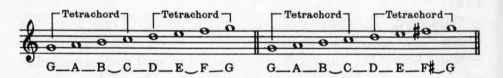

G __ A __ B ⌣ C __ D __ E ⌣ F __ G   G __ A __ B ⌣ C __ D __ E __ F♯ G

Key Signature. The sharps or flats occurring in a scale are grouped and placed to the right of the clef on the staff in the order of their appearance in the scale system. This grouping is called the key signature. For key signatures see pages 190, 194, 195, 196.

Some points to remember with regard to scales having sharps: (1) A new scale in sharps always begins on the fifth degree of the previous scale— a circle of fifths *ascending*. (2) A new scale retains all the sharps of the previous scale and adds one to the seventh tone. (3) To find the key-note from a signature in sharps remember that the last sharp added (the one farthest to the right) is on the seventh degree of the scale. Therefore, the note occupying the next line or space above will be the key-note.

The Scales and Keys having Flats. In explaining the construction of scales having sharps it was pointed out that by using the upper tetrachord of each scale as the first half of a new scale, a series of keys are formed having sharps, the tonic of each successive scale being the fifth tone of the previous scale. This procedure was based upon the facts stated in the foot-note on page 186. It was shown that the fifth above any given primary tone was the first different tone to appear in a series of overtones. Starting with C Major then, the scales having sharps are derived from an *ascending* circle of fifths.

C, the fifth tone above F, would be the first different tone to appear in a series of upper partial tones having F as a fundamental and for this reason

---

Suggestions for Scale Practice and Aural Drills to Establish Pitch Discrimination

For the teacher who has had little musical background but who wishes to have a thorough understanding of scale formations and to establish a feeling for tone relationships, the following procedure is recommended:

First establish the feeling for the tonic as the parent tone, the center toward which all other tones of the group tend to gravitate. To do this have someone play for you such exercises as those given below and verify your answers, either written or spoken. First have the assistant play a major scale slowly ascending and descending and then such tone groups as the following: 1 2 1, 1 3 1, 1 2 3 2 1, 1 3 2 3 1, 1 3 4 2 1, 1 2 4 3 1, 3 1 2 4 3, 1 4 2 3 1; 1 2 3 5 4, 5 1 2 4 3, 1 3 5 2 3, 5 3 1 2 3, 3 5 1 4 2, 3 4 2 5 1; 1 3 5 6 5, 1 2 4 6 5, 3 5 6 4 3, 1 6 4 2 1, 3 1 4 6 5, 1 3 6 3 5; 1 5 6 7 8, 1 3 5 7 8, 1 5 6 8 5, 3 1 6 4 8, 5 7 6 4 3, 8 5 3 2 1; 1 8 4 6 3, 8 6 7 5 8, 8 3 2 5 1, 1 8 7 5 8, 5 3 2 7 8.

A pause should be made after each group so that there will be time for you to write or recite them. Frequent changes of key are advisable, but each time the key is changed the new scale should be played before proceeding with tone groups so that the new tonic and the tonal relationships based upon it may be sensed.

Another extremely valuable procedure is to give yourself mental practice in "spelling" scales, that is, to give the letter names of tones of various scales. It is best to first give the letter names of the tones involved without regard to accidentals. Then go over the letters a second time, adding the sharps and flats wherever necessary to form the correct succession of intervals. Bear in mind that the intervals between E and F and between B and C are natural half-steps. It is well to practice the recitation of key signatures, taking care to name the sharps and flats in the order of their appearance in the scale system. Writing the scales is also good practice, and it is suggested that the bass and treble staves be used alternately. Observe the rules pertaining to the placing of stems on notes as given on page 186.

When you have made fair progress with ear training based upon the major scale, use the same type of exercise based upon the minor scale (harmonic form). This drill may also be continued by using the melodies of simple songs and piano pieces. Accidentals may be expressed by such terms as "3 flatted," "4 sharped," et cetera, and pitches above the octave by 9, 10, 11, et cetera.

After some practice in naming tone groups you will undoubtedly be strongly impressed with the attraction between the scale tones for each other and to the tonic. The dominant, leading tone, and supertonic are powerfully drawn to the tonic by direct progression such as 5-1, 5-8, 7-8, 2-1, or 5-7-8, 7-5-8, 7-9-8, 5-9-8. The mediant (the tone which gives the major or minor quality to a scale and key), the sub-dominant, and the sub-mediant progress to the tonic in various ways such as the following: 3-2-1, 3-4-2-1, 4-2-3-1, 6-5-8, 6-7-8.

The Major Scales

F was included in our original scale instead of F♯. It is evident that by *descending* in a circle of fifths an entirely new series of keys are secured. These are the keys having flats.

Reversing the procedure followed in forming the scales having sharps, by taking the *first* tetrachord of the scale of C (C—D—E⌣F) to form the *second* half of a new scale, and adding a new tetrachord below, the following scale results: F—G—A—B ⌣ C—D—E⌣F. It is necessary to place a flat before the fourth note in order to have the proper succession of intervals in each tetrachord (whole-step, whole-step, half-step). For the sake of convenience in writing, the tetrachord, C—D—E⌣F, is placed one octave higher in the new scale.

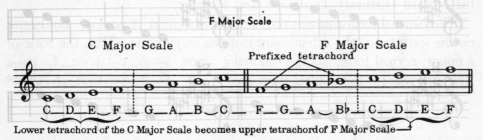

F Major Scale

C Major Scale   F Major Scale
                                             Prefixed tetrachord

C⌣D⌣E⌣F⌣G⌣A⌣B⌣C⌣   F⌣G⌣A⌣B♭⌣C⌣D⌣E⌣F

Lower tetrachord of the C Major Scale becomes upper tetrachord of F Major Scale

Some points to remember with regard to scales having flats: (1) A new scale in flats always begins on the fifth degree below the tonic of the previous scale (the same letter-name as the fourth degree above the tonic)— a circle of fifths *descending*. (2) A new scale retains all flats of the previous scale and adds one to the *fourth* tone. (3) To find the key-note from a signature in flats remember that the last flat added (the one farthest to the right) is on the fourth degree of the scale. Therefore the note occupying the line or space four degrees below is the key-note.

The Minor Scale. It has already been stated that the tone which determines the major or minor quality of a scale is the third tone. In the scale of C* for instance, the third tone is E. The interval between the tonic, C, and the mediant, E, is *four* half-steps or two whole-steps. The third tone in the scale of c minor is e♭ and the interval between the tonic, c, and the mediant, e♭, is *three* half-steps or one whole-step and one half-step. The effect of major and minor may be contrasted by sounding simultaneously on the piano the tones C - E - G, and then the tones c - e♭ - g.

*Capital letters are used when referring to major keys or scales, and small letters when referring to minor keys or scales; also in naming chords and intervals.

The terms *Relative minor* and *Relative major* are employed to express the close relationship existing between major and minor scales and keys which use the same signatures. The tonic of the relative minor of any major scale or key is on the sixth tone (or the third below the tonic) of the major scale.

Minor scales have no signatures of their own but use the signatures of the major scales on their third degrees. Thus, the scale of a minor has no sharps or flats in its signature because the relative major scale (C) beginning on its third degree has none. Likewise, c minor has the same signature as Eb Major because eb is the third tone in the scale of c minor.

Forms of the Minor Scale.   There are three forms of the minor scale, the Normal (natural), Harmonic, and Melodic.

The Normal form contains the same tones as its relative major but begins on the sixth tone (the sub-mediant) of the major scale. Thus the scale of a minor, normal form, has the following tones: a—b—c—d—e—f—g—a
The intervals for the natural form are: 1—2—3—4—5—6—7—8

Scale of a minor (Relative minor of C Major) Normal Form

la—ti—do—re—mi—fa—sol—la
1—2—3—4—5—6—7—8

The Harmonic form contains the same tones as the normal form except for the seventh tone which is one half-step higher in pitch. The scale of a minor in the harmonic form has the following tones:

a—b—c—d—e—f—g#—a
The intervals for the harmonic form are: 1—2—3—4—5—6—7—8

Scale of a minor (Relative minor of C Major) Harmonic Form

la—ti—do—re—mi—fa—si—la
1—2—3—4—5—6—7—8

The Melodic form contains the same tones as the normal form except for tones 6 and 7 which are each one half-step higher in the ascending scale but are restored to the normal form in the descending scale. The tones of the scale of a minor in the melodic form *ascending* are:

$$a—b—c—d—e—f\sharp—g\sharp—a$$

The intervals *ascending* are: 1—2—3—4—5—6 —7 —8
The tones *descending* are: a—g♮—f♮—e—d—c—b—a
The intervals *descending* are: 8—7 —6 —5—4—3—2—1

Scale of a minor (Relative minor of C Major) Melodic Form

la—ti—do—re—mi—fi—si—la   la—sol—fa—mi—re—do—ti—la
1 —2—3—4—5 —6—7—8   8 —7 —6 —5—4—3—2—1

Tonic Major and Tonic Minor.   When a major and a minor scale have the same tonic, the relationship between them is expressed as tonic major and tonic minor. Thus C Major is the tonic major of c minor and c minor the tonic minor of C Major.

Scale of c minor (Tonic minor of C Major) Melodic Form

la—ti—do—re—mi—fi—si—la   la—sol— fa—mi—re—do—ti—la
1—2—3—4—5—6—7—8   8 —7 — 6—5—4—3—2—1

Relative and tonic minors of the keys having sharps:

Tonic minor	c,	g,	d,	a,	e,	b,	f♯,	c♯
Major	C,	G,	D,	A,	E,	B,	F♯,	C♯
Relative minor	a,	e,	b,	f♯,	c♯,	g♯,	d♯,	a♯

Relative and tonic minors of the keys having flats:

Tonic minor	f,	b♭,	e♭,	a♭,	*(d♭)c♯	*(g♭)f♯	*(c♭)b
Major	F,	B♭,	E♭,	A♭,	D♭,	G♭,	C♭
Relative minor	d,	g,	c,	f,	b♭,	e♭,	a♭

*The tonic minors marked with an asterisk are not used by composers. Instead, the minors in sharps which begin on the same pitch (c♯ minor instead of d♭ minor, f♯ minor instead of g♭ minor, and b minor instead of c♭ minor) are used.

The Minor Scales

Comparison of intervals in the three forms of the minor.

Harmonic,

    ascending,   1—2‿3—4—5‿6—‿7‿8:   descends without change.

Normal (Natural)

    ascending,   1—2‿3—4—5‿6 — 7—8:   descends without change.

Melodic

    ascending,   1—2‿3—4—5—6 — 7‿8:

    descending, 8—7—6‿5—4—3 ‿ 2—1

Some points to remember with regard to the forms of the minor scales:
(1) The forms of the minor are alike in the first five tones, both ascending
and descending. (2) The normal and harmonic forms ascend and descend
without change. (3) The melodic form differs from the normal and harmonic forms ascending but only in tones six and seven. Descending it is the
same as the normal form.

Signatures of Relative Keys. The following chart shows the signatures
of major keys with their relative minor keys. Capital letters indicate major
and small letters indicate minor.

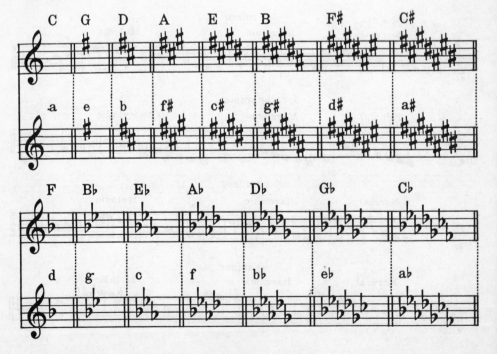

Enharmonic Scales.   The scales of B and Cb, F♯ and Gb, C♯ and Db, are called Enharmonic Scales because although different letter names are used, the same sounds are represented. Whenever a change of notation is made in a piece of music, as Ab instead of G♯, it is called an enharmonic change.

The Chromatic Scale.   The Chromatic scale, composed of half-steps exclusively, has twelve different pitches within the octave compared with but seven in the diatonic scales; all the tones of the diatonic scale are used together with the intervening tones.

In writing a chromatic scale the signature of the major scale of the starting tone should be observed. Ascending, the notes representing the intervening tones are written by raising chromatically numbers 1, 2, 4, 5, and 6 of the major scale; descending, the intervening tones are represented by chromatically lowering numbers 7, 6, 5, 3, and 2 of the major scale. Thus the chromatic scale from C is as follows: C C♯ D D♯ E F F♯ G G♯ A A♯ B C; descending, C B Bb A Ab G Gb F E Eb D Db C.

Examples of Chromatic Scales in Vocal Forms

Key of C Major

Key of E Major

Key of Eb Major

Rhythm and Meter

Origin of Rhythm. The power and necessity of rhythm was felt by man long before the fashioning of even the crudest musical instrument. Breathing, walking, running, the steady beat of waves on a shore and many other similar activities of man and nature provided the material from which this sense developed. The sense of rhythm is the source of some of the most profound and enduring satisfactions felt by man. The pleasure felt in all manifestations of symmetry, proportion, and order is rhythmic in origin. Arts as diverse as architecture, painting and sculpture are subservient to rhythmic law. It is of course a basic factor in music, poetry, and the dance, and a subject which has engrossed the attention of philosophers and thinkers of all time.

Fundamental Types of Rhythm. In visible nature the apprehension of beauty is through forms and colors, and in audible nature through rhythms and tones. Forms and their relations define space, and rhythms define time. The fundamental types of form are the straight line and the curve. The straight line is defined by two points and the curve by three. There are likewise but two fundamental types of rhythm, the duple and the triple defined by two and three beats respectively. A measure in duple rhythm, a meter of two, is expressed by two beats, the first being accented; a measure in triple rhythm, a meter of three, by three beats, the first being accented and the other two unaccented. The first beat or accent in a measure is the strongest. A measure in a meter of four beats is expressed as follows: strong, weak, medium-strong, weak—the equivalent of two duple measures. A measure of six beats may be expressed as a combination of three duple meters or two triple meters depending upon the nature and arrangement of the notes. The more unusual meters such as a meter of five and a meter of seven may be expressed respectively as a combination of a two and a three, and a three and a four. A single meter—a meter of one— is an impossibility because rhythm, like form, is based on proportion. A beat must be limited by a second beat before it can be a measure of time.

A word of explanation may be necessary regarding the use of the terms meter and beats in the preceding paragraph though it is believed the con- text has made the meaning clear. The word rhythm is used by many people to include every manifestation of motion and stress. To others its meaning is limited to the grouping of pulsations and does not apply to the duration of the sounds within a measure. To avoid confusion the word meter may be used to indicate the beat or pulsation-rhythm. In this sense meter is synonymous with the word "time" as when one speaks of the "time" of a composition. The expression "note-rhythm" may be used to indicate the characteristic arrangement of the notes within a measure—the duration of the sounds within the metric units. There can be no objection to the use of the word rhythm to express both the succession of pulsations or beats and the motion of the tones if the exact scope and shade of meaning is clearly shown.

Physical Expression of Rhythm. Laboratory experiment and observa-tion have confirmed the fact that our response to rhythm is physical rather than mental. The body vibrates to rhythms just as the delicate harp-like mechanism of the inner ear vibrates to sound. While this reaction to pulsa-tion is natural and our awareness of its effects more or less instinctive it is a sense that requires training before it can become a conscious element in the enjoyment of music. The more obvious reactions, such as are felt in hearing a band play a strong march rhythm, offer no particular difficulty to the average person. The more complex rhythms employed in a major orchestral composition for instance are often very perplexing to the untrained listener. Changes in tempo, accent points, and dynamics tend to weaken the listener's grasp of the meters and note-rhythms. Still more difficult to sense in their proper relations are the conjunctions of two opposed rhythms such as a duple and a triple within the same time unit. The failure of an accurate response to rhythms due to changes in tempo, accents, et cetera is often a mere lack of experience in listening rather than a poor feeling for rhythm. The student may find it hard to concentrate sufficiently and is confused by the multiplicity of elements which demand his attention.

With the gradual development of skill in pitch discrimination and the faculties associated with it the listener will find that he can turn his atten-tion at will to a consideration of either the melodic, harmonic, or rhythmic factors in a composition and still be able to hear it as a whole without the least strain or confusion. It should always be remembered that a mechanical accuracy in spacing the time intervals of beats is not necessarily an indication of a fine rhythmic perception. It will be noticed by the observant listener that in a really fine performance of a work there may be many subtle variations from strict metronomic accuracy and yet the impression is profoundly rhythmical and satisfying. This element of feeling is all-important. In addition to the measure rhythms already mentioned one should become conscious of phrase rhythms. These are much more flexible and various than measure rhythms and are made perfectly clear in the procedures beginning on page 211.

Time Signature (more correctly, Measure or Metric Signature). The term Time Signature is a misnomer because the word "time" as used in music is properly synonymous with the word tempo (speed) and refers to the rapidity with which the pulsations follow one another. In the absence of any general agreement on the use of a more precise term the common though mistaken usage will be followed in this chapter.

A time signature consists of two numbers placed one above the other on the staff to the right of the key signature. The upper number shows the beats in each measure and the lower number the kind of note or its equivalent occupying the time of one beat.

The numbers used to show the note values are as follows: 1, whole-note; 2, half-note; 4, quarter-note; 8, eighth-note; 16, sixteenth-note; 32, thirty-second note.

A broken circle similar to a large capital C sometimes found on the staff in place of the usual time signature indicates that the composition is to be performed in four-four measure or what is called Common Time. The same sign with a vertical line dividing it is called Alla Breve (äl-lä brav) indicating that the music, though written exactly as in four-four time, is to be performed more rapidly and give the impression of but two beats in each measure. It is commonly called "cut" time.

There are two types of measure, Simple and Compound. In Simple measure there is but one accent. All time signatures having 2 or 3 as the upper number are in Simple meter. All other signatures having 4, 6, 9, or 12 as the upper number, indicate Compound measure because in addition to the principal accent there are one or more secondary accents.

Normally the first beat of a measure receives the principal accent or stress.

The Most Common Meters

> indicates primary accent. **–** indicates principal secondary accent.

Syncopation. Syncopation is the irregular distribution of accents in music.

Triplets and Doublets. Whenever an irregular grouping of notes is used in a measure they are always indicated by a curved line (slur) and a number specifying how many notes are in the group. They are to be performed in a perfectly rhythmic manner so as to occupy the exact portion of time intended for them.

The most common of these irregular groupings are the triplet and the doublet.

A triplet is a group of three notes, each one of which is to occupy an equal portion of the time regularly given to two notes of the same value.

A doublet is a group of two notes, each one of which is to occupy an equal portion of the time regularly given to three notes of the same value.

Types of Measure. A measure of two beats is called duple measure, three beats triple measure, four beats quadruple measure, six beats sextuple measure. An almost infinite variety is possible in arranging the note and rest values to fill a given type of measure. See the illustration below giving a few measures in four-four, three-two, and six-eight.

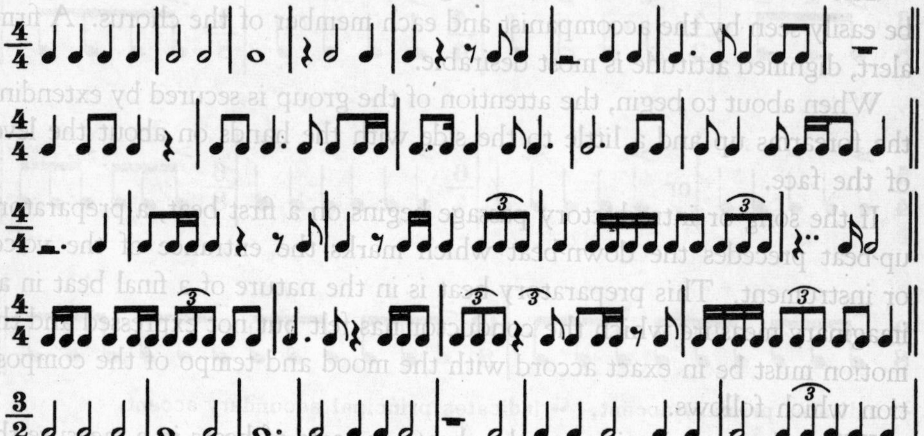

It is well to practice counting the beats aloud evenly and tapping each note of the illustrations given above. Adopt a slow "walking" tempo in all preliminary work and do but one group at a time. All difficult measures should be carefully analyzed and practiced separately. Follow this study by using any music available and tap the melodies in the same manner.

Conducting. In conducting group rehearsals of unfamiliar songs the teacher should be certain that the tempo, type of measure, and mood of the composition are clearly understood by the class before the singing is begun. After the song has been learned and (as a matter of course) in public performances preliminary counting aloud must not be resorted to.

The conductor should stand facing the singers in such a position as to be easily seen by the accompanist and each member of the chorus. A firm, alert, dignified attitude is most desirable.

When about to begin, the attention of the group is secured by extending the forearms up and a little to the side with the hands on about the level of the face.

If the song or introductory passage begins on a first beat, a preparatory up-beat precedes the down-beat which marks the entrance of the voices or instrument. This preparatory beat is in the nature of a final beat in an imaginary measure which the conductor has felt but not expressed and the motion must be in exact accord with the mood and tempo of the composition which follows.

When the piece begins on other beats or parts of beats in a measure the signal to begin is an *up* motion and *the beating of the measure is completed according to the motions indicated in the diagram given for that type of measure.* (See next page.)

The character of the motions employed varies in accordance with the type of music which is being performed but it should always be decisive, exact, and never wavering or indeterminate. The more vigorous and declamatory the music, the more forceful the beat of the conductor. The left hand and arm should be free to indicate nuances and special effects required while the right is occupied with the beats. The instant of ending the motion must coincide with the beat.

All measures felt in two beats are indicated as follows: (one) down, (two) up. All measures of three beats, (one) down, (two) right, (three) up. All measures of four beats, (one) down, (two) left, (three) right, (four) up. All measures of six beats, (one) down, (two three) left, (four) right, (five six) up.

It is usually more convenient and effective to conduct songs written in $\frac{4}{4}$ and $\frac{6}{8}$ as two-beat measures if the tempo is at all rapid. Under the same circumstances in measures of $\frac{3}{4}$ only the first beat of each measure is indicated. Measures of $\frac{9}{8}$ may be conducted according to the diagram given for the $\frac{3}{4}$ measure.

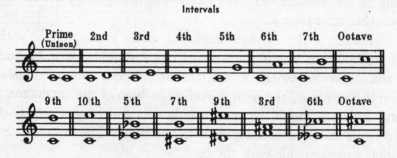

Intervals

An interval (the difference in pitch between two tones) may be either melodic or harmonic. Two tones sounded *successively* form a melodic interval and two tones sounded *simultaneously* form an harmonic interval.

Both the melodic and harmonic intervals are measured in the same way and have a number-name equal to the degrees of the staff they occupy counting from the lowest to the highest tone (both included). Thus from C to G is a fifth whether these tones are sounded successively or simultaneously because the interval between them is five degrees.

The number-names or general names of intervals are Primes or Unison, Seconds, Thirds, Fourths, Fifths, Sixths, Sevenths, Octaves, Ninths, and so on.

In addition to a general name, intervals also have specific names, as follows: Perfect, Major, Minor, Diminished, and Augmented. The major scale is the standard of measurement for all intervals.

An interval is **Perfect** when each of its tones is in the major scale which starts on the other tone. The fifth, C - G, is a perfect fifth because the tone C is in the major scale of G and the tone G is in the major scale of C.

An interval is **Major** when its upper tone is in the major scale starting on its lower tone. The third, C - E, is a major third because its upper tone E is in the scale of C Major.

An interval is **Minor** when it is less than a major by one-half step. The second, c - db, is a minor second because it is one half-step smaller than a major second (C - D).

An interval is **Diminished** when it is one half-step smaller than a minor or a perfect interval. The third, c# - eb, is a diminished third, being one half-step smaller than the minor third (c - eb). The fifth, c - gb, is a diminished fifth because it is one half-step smaller than the perfect fifth (C - G).

An interval is **Augmented** when it is one half-step larger than a major or a perfect interval. The second, C - D#, is an augmented second, the major second being C - D; the fourth, C - F#, is augmented, the perfect fourth being C - F. Obviously the fourth, Cb - F♮, is also augmented since the perfect fourth is Cb - Fb.

Simple and Compound Intervals. Simple intervals are intervals of an octave or less, while Compound intervals are intervals greater than an octave.

Compound intervals are classified according to the simple intervals to which they are related. The tenth, from middle C to E above the octave, for instance, is a compound major third because the simple interval C - E is a major third.

Consonant Intervals. A Consonant interval is a combination of two tones which by itself produces a complete and agreeable effect. Perfect octaves, fifths, and fourths are called Perfect Consonances, and the major and minor thirds and sixths are called Imperfect Consonances.

Dissonant Intervals. A Dissonant interval is a combination of two tones which produces an unsatisfactory incomplete effect and needs to be followed by another combination in which the dissonant tone is resolved. All seconds, sevenths, and augmented and diminished intervals are dissonant.

Resolution of a Dissonance. The process of following a dissonant interval with a consonant interval is called the Resolution of a dissonance.

The procedure given in the following will be helpful in acquiring aural ability in the recognition of intervals.

Interval Recognition. The classification of intervals must be based upon the lower tone as the tonic of a major scale. Make certain that the lower tone is clearly heard when two tones are sounded together. Make a careful study of the illustration of intervals on page 205. It will be observed that the following pairs of intervals sound alike; augmented primes and minor seconds; augmented seconds and minor thirds; major seconds and diminshed thirds; major thirds and diminished fourths; augmented fourths and diminished fifths; augmented fifths and minor sixths; major sixths and diminished sevenths; augmented sixths and minor sevenths. Therefore if the interval between two tones sounded is one whole-step and one half-step for instance it is correct to call it either an augmented second or a minor third.

Study the intervals within the octave of a major scale. It will be found that there are two sevenths (one major and one minor), three sixths (two major and one minor), four fifths (all perfect), five fourths (four perfect and one augmented), six thirds (three major and three minor), and seven seconds (five major and two minor).

Clearly distinguish the consonant intervals (concords) from the dissonant intervals (discords). It will be found that there are degrees of concord and of discord. The major third and minor sixth are the finest concords. Next in order come the minor thirds and major sixths, followed by the perfect fifths and fourths. Of the discords the major second and minor seventh are the least dissonant and the diminished fifth is also but slightly discordant. However, the major sevenths and minor seconds are harshly discordant. It will be of great assistance if these effects are carefully studied in connection with the interval drill which follows. Compare the major and minor thirds and sixths with the bare open quality of the perfect intervals, and the harsh dissonance of the minor seconds and major sevenths with the mild dissonance of the augmented fourth.

Following this preliminary work should come drill in the recognition of intervals through hearing alone. Secure the help of someone to play the intervals given below and to verify your answers, either written or spoken. The tones comprising each interval should first be sounded in succession from the lowest to the highest and then simultaneously. Hum or sing the two pitches and write or recite both its number name and its specific name. The key should be changed frequently but never without first playing the major scale slowly ascending and descending.

1-8, 1-5, 1-7, 1-5, 1-8; 1-5, 1-3, 1-5, 1-8; 1-8, 1-5, 1-3, 1-6, 1-5; 1-8, 1-4, 1-6, 1-3; 1-3, 1-5, 1-2, 1-4; 1-5, 3-5, 1-4, 2-4, 2-5, 1-5; 3-5, 3-8, 3-5, 2-6, 5-7, 3-8; 3-8, 1-6, 4-7, 4-5, 3-8; 3-5, 4-6, 2-7, 3-8; 7-8, 6-8, 5-7, 3-7, 2-8, 4-6, 1-5; 1-7, 3-4, 2-5, 3-7, 4-6, 3-8.

1-8, 3♭-8, 5-8, 2-7, 1-5, 3♭-5; 5-8, 5-7♭, 4-6, 4♯-6, 3-8; 1-5, 1-4♯, 2-4♯, 2-5, 1-3♭; 4♭-6, 5-7, 4-8, 3♭-5; 1-8, 3♭-8, 3♭-4♯, 2-5, 1-6♭, 4-7, 3♭-8; 3♭-8, 1-7, 3-7♭, 1-6, 3-4♯, 2-6, 1♯-3, 1-4; 4♯-6, 3♭-7, 2-8, 1♯-5, 1-3.

Chords

Chord. A chord is the simultaneous sounding of three or more tones. The tone from which a chord takes its rise is called the Root of the chord.

The tones of a chord in its root position are separated from each other by the interval of three degrees—a major or a minor third.

Triad. A triad is a three-toned chord consisting of a root or fundamental tone with its third and fifth above. The chord C-E-G is the tonic triad in the key of C, the tone C being called the root of the cord, E the third of the chord, and G the fifth of the chord. The fundamental quality of this chord as the tonic major triad in the key of C is not affected by placing any of the tones comprising it above or below the others.

If the tone C is the lowest tone when this triad is sounded, it is said to be in the root or first position regardless of whether E or G is the highest tone or in what octave above they may be placed.

If the tone E is the lowest tone when this triad is sounded it is said to be in the second position regardless of whether C or G is the highest tone or in what octave above they may be placed.

If the tone G is the lowest tone when this triad is sounded it is said to be in the third position regardless of whether E or C is the highest tone or in what octave above they may be placed.

The second and third positions of a triad are also called the Inversions of the chord, the first inversion being the *second position* and the second inversion the *third position*.

Formation and Classification of Triads. Triads may be formed on any degree of the diatonic scales and in all keys and are classified as Major, Minor, Diminished, and Augmented.

If a triad in the root position comprises the tones 1, 3, and 5 of a major scale based upon the fundamental tone, it is a *major* triad.

If a triad in the root position comprises the tones 1, 3, and 5 of a minor scale based upon the fundamental tone, it is a *minor* triad.

The triad on the sub-dominant in the key of C (F-A-C), is a *major* triad because the tones are 1, 3, and 5 in the scale of F Major; the triad on the mediant in the key of C (e-g-b) is a *minor* triad because the tones are 1, 3, and 5 of the scale of e minor.

The triad on the leading tone in both the major and minor scales (Harmonic Form) is a diminished triad.

The triad on the mediant of the minor scale (Harmonic Form) is an augmented triad.

In all *major* triads there are four half-steps (two whole-steps) between the root tone and its third, and three half-steps (one whole-step and one half-step) between the third and the fifth of the chord.

In all *minor* triads there are three half-steps between the root tone and its third, and four half-steps between the third and fifth of the chord.

In all *diminished* triads there are three half-steps between the root tone and its third, and three half-steps between the third and fifth of the chord.

In all *augmented* triads there are four half-steps between the root tone and its third, and four half-steps between the third and fifth of the chord.

In the illustrations given below the *chord positions* are indicated by *arabic numerals,* major and augmented triads by *large* roman numerals, and minor and diminished triads by *small* roman numerals.

Triads on the Tones of the Scale of C Major

GCE	adf	beg	CFA	DGB	eac	fbd
EGC	fad	gbe	ACF	BDG	cea	dfb
CEG	dfa	egb	FAC	GBD	ace	bdf
I(Major)	II(minor)	III(minor)	IV(Major)	V(Major)	VI(minor)	VII(diminished)

Triads on the Tones of the Scale of c minor

The triads illustrated on the preceding page are called the Diatonic Triads of a key.

All major scales contain three major triads (I, IV, V), three minor triads (II, III, VI), and one diminished triad (VII).

All minor scales (Harmonic form) contain two major triads (V, VI), two minor triads (I, IV), two diminished triads (II, VII) and one augmented triad (III).

Primary Triads. The triads on the tonic, dominant, and sub-dominant of the major and minor keys are called the Primary triads, and they include all the tones of their respective scales.

Chords of the Seventh. A Chord of the Seventh is a four-toned chord—a root tone with its third, fifth, and seventh above. The tones C-E-G-B sounded together form the tonic seventh chord in the key of C Major, the sub-dominant seventh chord in the key of G Major, and the sub-mediant seventh chord in the key of e minor.

A seventh chord may be written in four positions since it consists of four tones. If the root of the chord is the lowest tone it is in root position regardless of whether the third, fifth, or seventh of the chord is the highest tone. The same rule is applied to the second, third, and fourth positions of this chord. If the term "inversion" is used the second position is the first inversion, the third position is the second inversion, and the fourth position is the third inversion.

Dominant Seventh Chord. The most important of the seventh chords is the chord of the Dominant seventh. The tones comprising this chord are the same for each major key and its tonic minor. Thus in both C Major and c minor (Harmonic form) the dominant seventh chord consists of the tones g-b-d-f.

Dominant Seventh Chord

Ninth and Eleventh Chords. A Chord of the Ninth is a root tone with its third, fifth, seventh, and ninth above.

A chord of the Eleventh consists of a root tone with its third, fifth, seventh, ninth, and eleventh above.

Chromatic Chord.   If chromatic signs (sharps, flats, or naturals which do not belong in the key) are used in the notation of a chord it is called a Chromatic chord.

Harmony. Harmony is an agreeable combination of tones simultaneously heard. It is also the science and art of combining tones of different pitch and the study of the laws governing the reciprocal relations between chords.

Modulation.   The transition from one key to another in a piece of music is called Modulation. To effect a modulation it is necessary to introduce one or more altered tones (by means of chromatic signs) which create the feeling of a new tonic and a new system of tonal relationships. If the change of key is temporary the original signature is usually retained.

Cadence.   A cadence is a chord progression which marks the end of a composition or of a definite portion of a composition. The feeling of cadence is analogous to the need for punctuation in writing or speaking. When accurately used the term cadence refers only to the two final chords.

The only completely satisfactory chord upon which a composition may end is the tonic chord in root position. The tonic chord is usually preceded by either a chord on the dominant or the sub-dominant also in the root position. However at other cadential points in a piece of music the cadence may end upon various chords.

If the final chord of a cadence is the tonic and it is preceded by one of the other primary triads also in root position it is called a Full Cadence. (See 1, 2, 3 in illustration.)

Cadences

If the cadence ends on the chord of the dominant it is called a Half-Cadence. (See 4 and 5 in illustration.)

If the final chord of the cadence is neither the tonic nor dominant chord but is preceded by the chord on the dominant it is called a Deceptive Cadence. (See 6 in illustration.)

Consonant Chord. A consonant chord is a group of tones which make consonant intervals with each other. The triad C-E-G is a consonance because it contains a major third (C-E), a minor third (e-g), and a perfect fifth (C-G), all of which are consonant intervals. (See page 205 for examples of consonant intervals.)

Dissonant Chord. A dissonant chord consists of tones which do not make consonant intervals with each other. For example, the dominant seventh chord in the key of C (G-B-D-F) contains a major third (G-B), two minor thirds (b-d and d-f), and a perfect fifth (G-D) all of which are consonant intervals. But the other intervals it contains, the minor seventh (g-f) and the diminished fifth (b-f) are both dissonant intervals. Therefore the dominant seventh chord is a dissonance—a chord requiring resolution.

Passing Tones. Tones not belonging to the chord with which they are sounded and used in a progression scale-wise from one chord to another are called Passing Tones.

> The first two sixteenth-notes in the second measure of the *Marching Song*[1] represent passing tones since the tonic chord in the key of F (F - A - C) forms the basic harmony and the notes referred to (both are G's) do not belong in that chord. The notes immediately preceding and following the passing notes are however in each instance tones belonging to the chord.

Transposition. The writing or performance of a composition in a different key from the one originally employed is called a Transposition.

ELEMENTS OF FORM

Motive. A motive is a short, trenchant, musical figure which forms the germ or seed from which a composition is developed. It may consist of but two or three notes and is rarely more than two measures in length.

> A splendid example of a motive may be found in the first three notes of the introduction to *The Blacksmith*[2] by Mozart. The repetition of the rhythmic and melodic features of this motive is a characteristic of the entire song.

Phrase and Section or Semi-phrase. A phrase is a musical idea normally two or four measures in length ending in a cadence. There are also many instances of irregular types found particularly in modern music such as phrases having three, five, six, seven, eight or nine measures. In general, the length of the phrase is determined by the signature and the rate of movement of the composition. If the signature is $\frac{4}{4}$, $\frac{6}{8}$, $\frac{9}{8}$, or $\frac{12}{8}$ and the

---

[1]p. 170, [2]No. 129, The Silver Book of Songs—Victor Record 20739.

tempo indicated is moderate or slow the phrases are most often but two measures long. But if the measures contain but two or three beats and the tempo is rapid, the phrases will usually be four measures in length and may even have eight or more measures.

The phrase is the structural unit which is the basis of all musical form and the smallest element of form capable of giving satisfactory expression to a musical thought.

> The song Bow, Wow, Wow![3] is four measures, one phrase in length, and a clear feeling of "punctuation" will be observed which divides the song into two *sections* or *semi-phrases,* the first section being measures 1 - 2, and the second, measures 3 - 4.

Period. The period is a complete musical statement usually four or eight measures in length and composed of two phrases. It is subject to the conditions and exceptions mentioned as governing the length of the phrase such as tempo and signature.

Antecedent and Consequent. The two phrases of the normal period are called respectively Antecedent and Consequent.

> Old Black Joe[4] is one of the numerous examples of the two measure phrase and the four-measure period. The entire song is three periods in length—two in the first part and one in the chorus. Notice that the tempo is slow (poco adagio) and the signature $\frac{4}{4}$ Measures one and two constitute the antecedent phrase, and measure three and four the consequent phrase of the first period. The sections of each phrase are also very clearly defined in this song, illustrating one of the most important principles of design—repetition. The feeling of structural unity is enhanced by many similarities in melody, harmony, and rhythm between the phrases and periods. The antecedent of the first period is exactly the same as the antecedent of the second period. The consequent phrase of the second period is repeated at the end of the third period (chorus) and the second section of the first phrase is repeated in each period of the song: Study this song carefully in the light of the analysis just given.
>
> The four-measure phrase and the eight-measure period are illustrated in a great many simple songs including Autumn Leaves[5], In September[6], The Man in the Moon[7], and Cold's the Wind[8]. The sections or semi-phrases are very apparent in The Bells[9] where measures 1 - 2 and 3 - 4 are two distinct parts of the first phrase. There is a similar arrangement in the second phrase of this song (measures 5 - 8).

Irregular Phrases and Periods. Compositions containing periods and phrases irregular in construction are met with quite frequently. A good example is America[10] in which the first period is six measures long and the second, eight measures long. When Morning Gilds the Skies[11] is thirteen measures long, the first period having six, and the second, seven measures.

[3]p. 103, [4]p. 136, [5]p. 101, [6]p. 101, [7]p. 101, [8]p. 129, [9]p. 116, [10]p. 145, [11]No. 169, The Silver Book of Songs —Victor Record 22626.

Every aspect—melodic, harmonic, rhythmic, and formal—of these two songs is in such perfect accord with the texts that analysis of them in some detail may be interesting and instructive.

Each verse of *America* contains seven lines and is divisible into two parts, the first containing lines one to three and the second, lines four to seven. These parts always end with a period or exclamation point indicating a full stop—the end of a complete statement. Reciting the words rhythmically reveals that each line is felt in two measures of three beats each or fourteen measures for an entire verse. The melody and harmony required to express this verse must therefore not only accord with its dignity and elevation of thought, and the rhythm of its lines, but also with its natural divisions.

In examining the music one finds these requirements have been met. A fine, broad, compact melody supported by simple, majestic harmonies (for the most part the chords are in root position) provides a splendid setting for the words. The measure signature is $\frac{3}{4}$ and the expression mark, maestoso. Each line of the verse is expressed in two measure phrases. The periods, the one ending with measure six (the end of line three of the verse), and the other ending with measure fourteen (the end of line seven of the verse) exactly accord with the two divisions of the verse. Full cadences mark the end of these periods, the cadence ending the second period being the most compelling. Four of the seven phrases in the song have the same rhythmic basis.

In *When Morning Gilds the Skies* the first period (six measures) contains three two measure phrases while the second (seven measures) contains two phrases of two measures each and one of three measures. The verse is of six lines and its rhythmic character is such as to be normally expressed in two six-measure periods. However the composer wished to create a greater feeling of climax in the final phrase and this was achieved by expanding it through the use of half-notes instead of the quarter-note values prevailing in the other phrases. The first period ends in a half-cadence.

Important. In determining the structure of a composition always begin counting with the *first full measure* of the voice part in the case of songs, or of the melody in instrumental compositions. Thus introductory measures and also parts of measures at the beginning of a composition when the melody starts on a beat other than the first are not considered in figuring the length of a phrase or period. However if the last measure is not complete it is counted as a full measure.

BIBLIOGRAPHY

For the teacher who wishes to make a more detailed study of the rudiments of music and would like some good reference works in the history of music the following are recommended:

Musical Theory, Books One and Two and Teacher's Manual, Arthur Olaf Anderson—H. T. FitzSimons Co., Chicago.
Student's Harmony Book, Preston Ware Orem—Clayton F. Summy Co., Chicago.

Musical Forms, Ernst Pauer—Oliver Ditson Co., Boston.
Ear Training for Teacher and Pupil, C. A. Alchin—Oliver Ditson Co., Boston.
Elementary Theory and Practice, Robert Bartholomew—Theodore Presser Co., Philadelphia.
Elementary Music Theory, Robert Fisher Smith—Oliver Ditson Co., Boston.
Musical Essentials, Harold Maryott—Theodore Presser Co., Philadelphia.
Elson's Music Dictionary, Louis C. Elson—Oliver Ditson Co., Boston.
The Story of Music, Paul Bekker—W. W. Norton & Co., New York.
The Study of the History of Music, Edward Dickinson—Charles Scribner's Sons, New York.
The History of Music, Cecil Gray—Alfred A. Knopf, New York.
The History of Music, Waldo Selden Pratt—G. Schirmer, Inc., New York.
A History of Music, Theodore M. Finney—Harcourt, Brace & Co., New York.
An Outline of the History of Music, Karl Nef—Columbia University Studies in Musicology No. 1, Columbia University Press, New York.

INDEX OF TEXT

(See also Index of Songs on page 216.)

INDEX OF SONGS